Public Matters

Public Matters

Essays on Politics, Policy and Religion

William A. Galston

ROWMAN & LITTLEFIELD PUBLISHERS, INC.
Lanham • Boulder • New York • Toronto • Oxford

ROWMAN & LITTLEFIELD PUBLISHERS, INC.

Published in the United States of America
by Rowman & Littlefield Publishers, Inc.
A wholly owned subsidary of The Rowman & Littlefield Publishing Group, Inc.
4501 Forbes Boulevard, Suite 200, Lanham, Maryland 20706
www.rowmanlittlefield.com

PO Box 317
Oxford
OX2 9RU, UK

British Library Cataloguing in Publication Information Available

Library of Congress Cataloging-in-Publication Data

Galston, William A. (William Arthur), 1946–
   Public matters : essays on politics, policy, and religion / William A. Galston.
    p. cm.
   Includes bibliographical references and index.
   ISBN 0-7425-4979-8 (cloth : alk. paper)—ISBN 0-7425-4980-1 (pbk. : alk. paper)
   1. United States—Politics and government—2001– 2. Political planning—United
   States. 3. Religion and politics—United States. I. Title.
   JK275.G35 2005
   320.6'0973'090511—dc22   2005008940

Printed in the United States of America

∞™ The paper used in this publication meets the minimum requirements of American
National Standard for Information Sciences—Permanence of Paper for Printed Library
Materials, ANSI/NISO Z39.48-1992.

Contents

Acknowledgments

The Introduction and Chapter 10 are appearing for the first time. The remaining chapters have been published previously, as follows: Chapter 1 as "Incomplete Victory: The Rise of the New Democrats," in Peter Berkowitz, ed., *Varieties of Progressivism in America* (Stanford, CA: Hoover Institution, 2004); Chapter 2 as "Democrats Adrift?," *The Public Interest* 157 (Fall 2004); Chapter 3 as "The Long View: Why the GOP keeps winning," *Commonweal*, December 3, 2004, and "Moral Values and the U.S. Election," *America*, February 14, 2005; Chapter 4 as "Civil Society and the 'Art of Association'," *Journal of Democracy* 11, 1 (January 2000); Chapter 5 as "The Perils of Preemption," *The American Prospect*, September 22 2002; Chapter 6 as "Thinking About the Draft," *The Public Interest* 154 (Winter 2004); Chapter 7 as "Ethics and Public Policy in a Democracy: The Case of Human Embryo Research," in Arthur W. Galston and Emily G. Shurr, eds., *New Dimensions in Bioethics: Science, Ethics, and the Formulation of Public Policy* (Boston: Kluwer, 2001); Chapter 8 as "Observations on Some Proposals to Help Parents: A Progressive Perspective," in Sylvia Ann Hewlett, Nancy Rankin, and Cornel West, eds., *Taking Parenting Public: The Case for a New Social Contract* (Lanham, MD: Rowman & Littlefield, 2002); Chapter 9 as "The Case of Frankfurter v. Jackson," *The Public Interest* 155 (Spring 2004); Chapter 11 as "Contending with Liberalism," in Margaret O'Brien Steinfels, ed., *American Catholics and Civic Engagement: A Distinctive Voice* (Lanham, MD: Rowman & Littlefield, 2004); Chapter 12 as "Traditional Judaism and American Citizenship," in Alan Mittleman, ed., *Religion as a Public Good: Jews and Other Americans on Religion in the Public Square* (Lanham, MD: Rowman & Littlefield, 2003); and Chapter 13 as "Jews, Muslims, and the prospects for pluralism," *Daedalus* (Summer 2003).

I am grateful to the respective publishers and editors for permission to reprint.

Introduction

During the past quarter century I have lived an unusual double life. I have plied the trade for which I was trained, as a political theorist based in academia. And I have participated in American politics, as a policy intellectual, campaign aide, party reformer, and White House official. Each of these lives has shaped the others in ways that I have only begun to understand: my political theorizing has framed the way I view concrete political life, and my political entanglements have reshaped the way I do political theory.

For more than two years, I served as issues director in Walter F. Mondale's presidential campaign. His forty-nine-state defeat at the hands of Ronald Reagan forced me to wonder whether the public's verdict was simply a personal victory for the charismatic Great Communicator. Four years later, the come-from-behind victory of the decidedly uncharismatic George H. W. Bush over Michael Dukakis added urgency to these reflections, and I joined forces with others who were struggling against long odds to renovate the Democratic Party.

The essays gathered in Part I of this volume were written in the shadow of this struggle. They offer my interpretation of the principles that guided us, and of the consequences of our efforts. They reflect, as well, two other conclusions that I came to hold more and more firmly during this period. First, politics in large modern societies is more than a matter of short-term tactics, coalitions, or spin. Long-cycle changes in circumstances, demography, and public culture define the arena within which political competition proceeds. Parties that grasp and can respond to these changes tend to prevail; those that do not become all but irrelevant. Second, modern politics is more than individuals vying for public endorsement on the basis of their personal strengths. Institutions—legislatures, bureaucracies, and parties, among others—play critical roles as the venues within which differences can be sharpened and collective judgments reached.

Some public debate concerns first principles of morality, but more revolves around the classic political question: what should we do? The second section of this volume offers a sample of the public policy debates, domestic and international, in which I have participated. While we can almost never derive policy positions from moral premises, we cannot ignore the moral dimension of policy conflict. Nor can we ignore the morally expressive function of the laws that encode the outcome of this conflict.

At the same time, public deliberation will not go well in the absence of the relevant facts and causal linkages, fairly and rigorously assessed. Many public conflicts that seem at first to be predominantly moral turn out to be highly dependent on empirical claims. Consider the debate over stem cell research that became prominent in the 2004 presidential campaign. As public opinion shifted, President Bush felt compelled to deploy his wife. Laura Bush joined, not the moral debate about the status of the pre-embryo, but rather the empirical debate about the prospects of stem cells in the battle against dread diseases. In so doing, she recognized the deliberative force of claims that will be verified or falsified by medical researchers rather than theologians and moral philosophers.

At this point, readers may start to wonder whether my practical activities represent, not an expression of my theorizing, but rather a parallel life that does not intersect it. To address this doubt, I must now cast a wider net.

Over the past decade, I have come to defend a conception of political life that I call liberal pluralist democracy. It is liberal in that I insist that the scope of rightful political authority is limited. It is pluralist, first, because I have come to believe that the things we have reason to value are heterogeneous and irreducible to a common measure; and second, because the political sphere is but one of multiple, mutually limiting sources of legitimate authority. And it is democratic because I am more willing to wager the outcome of politics on the collective will of the people than on any of the alternatives; not that the people are right in every case, or in the short term, but rather for the most part, over time.[1]

As I have developed this understanding of decent politics, I have encountered a deep tension, in my thinking and in the world. On the one hand, liberal pluralist democracy is a politics of freedom: it places what I call expressive liberty—the ability of individuals and groups to live in the ways that enact their diverse conceptions of what gives meaning and value to their lives—at the core of the enterprise of politics. On the other hand, a liberal pluralist democracy cannot sustain itself solely through artfully arranged institutions. It requires, as well, citizens with distinctive beliefs, dispositions, and loyalties. The partisans of liberal pluralist democracy must pay attention, therefore, to the processes, formal and informal—civic education, civil associations, family, culture, and faith—through which human beings become such citizens.

The difficulty is that, in practice, the policies that nudge the formative effects of these institutions in pro-civic directions can collide with the exercise of expressive liberty. I have discovered no bright-line principle that neatly adjudicates these conflicts. To remain both decent and sustainable, a liberal pluralist democracy must manage them without falling either into the extreme of a libertarianism that is blind to the requisites of citizenship or into its opposite, a civic republicanism that gives short shrift to individual and associational liberty.

As a younger scholar, I analyzed religion in neo-Tocquevillian functionalist terms, as a source of support for democratic principles and as a crucible for forging democratic citizenship. Today, I see religion through the prism of the ambiguous relations among civic life, expressive liberty, and multiple sources of authority. We cannot adequately understand religion as civic, because many (not all) faiths assert claims to authority that limit the scope of politics. Nor is there any guarantee that the kinds of individuals we tend to become under the influence of various faith traditions will embrace the requirements of citizenship. Theorists as diverse as Machiavelli and Rousseau saw an outright contradiction between the teachings of Christianity and devotion to civic life. Their response to this conundrum (pagan virtue in Machiavelli's case, civil religion in Rousseau's) defined the poles between which much political theory has since oscillated. The pluralist alternative—the uneasy, non-hierarchic coexistence of political and religious authority urged by British thinkers such as J. N. Figgis and Reformed Calvinists led by Abraham Kuyper—has remained a neglected minority view within mainstream political theory. In the concluding section, I explore this issue as it emerges in diverse cultural contexts and faith traditions.

The essays in this volume trace an itinerary of public engagement. As such, they are concrete and historically situated. Many seek to shape events as they unfold; some offer conjectures about the consequences of decisions yet to be made at the time of their publication. While I have corrected minor infelicities of tone and have edited some of the chapters to avoid needless overlaps, I have made no effort to revise the record. Readers can see and judge for themselves the extent to which my predictions turned out to be accurate and my recommendations, prudent.

After a quarter century of public engagement, I have concluded that there is no contradiction between the systematic effort to understand the world as it is and a deep determination to make it better. Quite the contrary: criticism is useless unless the critic is prepared to offer an alternative and fight for it. Abstract possibilities untethered from considerations of feasibility may stir the passions and fire the imagination, but they are unlikely to improve the well-being of one's fellow citizens, or of humanity.

The significance of political reality extends, or ought to extend, beyond the world of practice. I see no point in drafting utopias inhabited by beings purer, or baser, than what human beings can be at their best or worst. Political theory that does not emerge from, or reflect on, the real world of politics is at best a mandarin exercise, an inward-looking sphere of discourse that need detain no one save its hermetic devotees.

NOTES

1. For the full story, see my *Liberal Pluralism* (New York: Cambridge University Press, 2002) and *The Practice of Liberal Pluralism* (New York: Cambridge University Press, 2004).

Part I

POLITICS

Chapter One

Incomplete Victory: The Rise of the New Democrats (2004)

THE DYNAMICS OF PARTY CHANGE

My task in this chapter is to explain the rise and significance of the New Democratic movement within the Democratic Party. Because this is an instance of a more general phenomenon—party change—I begin with some broad reflections on the dynamics of party change in the United States.

In one of their few notable failures of insight, the drafters of the U.S. Constitution did not foresee that the electoral system they constructed had created incentives for the formation of political parties and pressures to consolidate factions into a small number of major aggregations. Through most of the past two centuries, American politics has been dominated by competition between two principal parties; for the past century and one half, between the same two parties. With but a few exceptions (the collapse of the Federalists and Whigs, the rise of the Republicans), political change has taken place through changes within established parties.

As one reflects on the history of intra-party change in the United States, four sources emerge as key. The first is the simple logic of party competition. In many respects, our political system is much closer to winner-take-all than are most parliamentary systems. Members of political parties have strong incentives, therefore, to settle for nothing less than victory. A string of defeats at the hands of the opposition will generate pressures for change. For example, Dwight Eisenhower's "Modern Republicanism" reflected the recognition that the New Deal had become a permanent feature of American politics and that continued opposition to it would consign Republicans to irrelevance. Another source of competitive pressure is the rise of third parties that threaten to erode existing majorities or to thwart the formation of new ones. Republicans dealt far more successfully with the 1968 insurgency of George Wallace than did Democrats, while Democrats dealt more successfully with Ross Perot's challenge in 1992. In both cases, the result was multiple victories in presidential contests.

Fundamental shifts in the economy and society constitute a second principal source of party change. The post–Civil War shift from agriculture and individual entrepreneurship to large corporations and mass production created stresses and opportunities on which the Republican Party was able to capitalize, culminating in the realigning election of 1896. Demographic shifts, whether generated externally through immigration or internally through large birth cohorts, create political opportunities—namely, substantial pools of potential new voters with distinctive concerns.

A third source of change takes the form of shocks—events that produce a rupture with the past and to which political parties are compelled to respond. Two classic examples are the Great Depression, which opened the door to an enlarged and restructured national government, and Pearl Harbor, which ended the debate between isolationists and internationalists that had dominated the interwar period. By taking the side of big government at home and robust engagement abroad, Democrats captured the political high ground and held it for two generations. (The current Bush administration is doing everything it can to make the case that September 11 represents another such transformative external shock.)

Sometimes these reorienting shocks originate within the political system itself. During the past fifty years, for example, Supreme Court decisions on school integration, school prayer, and abortion have forced both parties to respond. It would not have been easy for political observers in 1954 to predict that Democrats would become the party of civil rights, reproductive choice, and strict separation between church and state. But so it proved, and in the process the dynamics of party competition were transformed.

What I call redefining ideas constitute a final source of party change. Ideas enter the political system through two routes, which might be stylized as bottom-up and top-down. Throughout the 20th century, popularly based social movements conveyed ideas to political parties. Civil rights, women's rights, prohibition, and environmentalism are instances drawn from a very long list. In other cases, however, scholars and policy activists without a popular base can directly influence party elites. Herbert Croly's *The Promise of American Life* influenced two generations of progressive leaders. Keynesian economics, which reconfigured the Democratic Party, and supply-side economics, which did the same for Republicans, were in the main transactions between elites that generated, rather than being generated by, popular movements.

Before turning to a detailed examination of the rise of the New Democrats, let me use the four-fold template of party change I have sketched to characterize, in broad brush-strokes, the forces the fueled the movement. There can be no doubt, to begin, that inter-party competition was a major motivation. The New Democratic movement began to take shape in the immediate wake of Walter Mondale's defeat. Between 1968 and 1984, Democrats lost four of five presidential elections, two by historic landslides. And Michael Dukakis's 1988 loss to George H. W. Bush propelled New Democrats into a far more aggressive stance within their party.

Socioeconomic change played a smaller but still perceptible role. During the early 1980s, the emergence of a technology based post-industrial and service economy led some Democrats to wonder whether New Deal policies and arrangements, rooted as they were in mass industrial production, would serve either the country or the party well in the late 20th century.

Transformative shocks played almost no role in the rise of the New Democrats. In contrast to many other episodes of party change, it is hard to point to a pivotal event in the economy, in the international arena, or even in the judicial system. To be sure, the fall of the Berlin Wall and the collapse of communism were momentous, but they had a remarkably small impact on the substance of New Democrats' policy development, and not much more on their political fortunes. Or so I shall argue.

Finally, New Democrats worked with some success to use redefining ideas as a source of political change. But perhaps fatefully, these ideas entered the political system from the top rather than the bottom. Unlike (say) the Goldwater-Reagan transformation of the Republican Party, New Democrats did not rely on, and for some time did little to create, a grass-roots movement of committed activists. As a result, Bill Clinton, the quintessential New Democratic standard-bearer, prevailed in the 1992 presidential election on the strength of ideas that enjoyed wider acceptance among the people as a whole than they did within his own party. The contrast between the fractious executive-legislative relations during the first two years of Clinton's presidency and the disciplined inter-branch cooperation during the first two years of George W. Bush's is stark.

THE HISTORICAL CONTEXT: PARTY CHANGE, 1961–1980

My thesis in this section is that profound changes within both political parties from the inauguration of John F. Kennedy to the election of Ronald Reagan laid the political predicate for the emergence of the New Democratic movement. Let me begin with the Democrats.

Economics.   Kennedy took office determined to accelerate economic
growth after the two recessions in Eisenhower's second term, and he was
confident that growth would promote the general welfare. After all, he remarked, "A rising tide lifts all boats." At the same time, his encounter with
poverty during the West Virginia primary had shocked and moved him.
One of his earliest legislative proposals was the Area Redevelopment Act,
targeted on Appalachia. By emphasizing measures such as the War on
Poverty, Lyndon Johnson more fully associated Democrats with the redis-
tributive dimension of economic policy. Under the control of George Mc-
Govern's forces, the 1972 Democratic convention drafted the most aggres-
sively redistributionist platform in the party's recent history. For his part,
Jimmy Carter came close to challenging the very desirability of growth by
associating his administration with stringent energy conservation and the
"limits to growth" thesis popularized by the Club of Rome. Meanwhile,
soaring inflation weakened public confidence in his stewardship of the
economy. By the election of 1980, the link between the Democratic Party
and economic growth had frayed.

Defense and foreign policy.   During the 1960 election, John F. Kennedy ran
to Nixon's right on defense and foreign policy, charging that the Eisenhower administration had failed to prosecute the Cold War with vigor and
had allowed a "missile gap" to develop with the Soviet Union. His Cold
War liberalism combined support for international institutions and law with
a willingness to use force on behalf of American interests and values. The
Vietnam War shattered this consensus by driving a wedge between international engagement and the deployment of power. The 1972 Democratic
platform called, not only for unilateral U.S. withdrawal from Vietnam, but
also for troop cuts in Europe, steep reductions in military expenditures, and
an end to the draft. While more moderate in tone and substance, the 1976
Democratic platform advocated cutting weapons systems, reducing reliance on military force as an instrument of foreign policy, and emphasizing the pursuit of human rights rather than the traditional concerns of *re-
alpolitik*. The Carter administration's inability to resolve its internal
disputes about relations with the Soviets and ambivalence about the use of
force contributed to a series of overseas reverses and raised public doubts
about the Democratic Party's stewardship of defense and foreign policy.

Social and cultural issues.   During the 1960s and 1970s, the Democratic
Party's orientation on social and cultural issues underwent a profound
transformation. The party moved from ambivalence and division to a
wholehearted embrace of civil rights for African Americans. It moved from
a male-dominated organization in which women's rights and concerns
were given short shrift to the endorsement of legalized abortion and the

Equal Rights Amendment. The party's views on crime and criminal justice reflected a shift away from punishment towards sociological explanations ("root causes") and alternatives to incarceration. Once squarely rooted in the cultural mainstream, the party opened itself to the counterculture, most conspicuously at its 1972 convention, whose platform endorsed the "right to be different." And with increasing fervor, Democrats embraced a legal-istically strict separation of church and state, creating at least the perception of a basically secularist orientation.

Stance toward government. At the core of the New Deal outlook was a deep faith in government, as the local of public-spirited action and as the most effective vehicle for accomplishing a wide range of collective tasks. Despite some tonal novelties, the Kennedy administration shared that faith. By the Carter administration, that faith had mutated into something close to its opposite. Under the impact of Vietnam and Watergate, trust in the es-sential integrity of government had been replaced by the presumption of self-serving venality and dishonesty. And substantial portions of the party had shifted from confidence in government as the engine of social and eco-nomic reform to deep ambivalence. In his 1978 State of the Union address, Jimmy Carter said:

> Government cannot solve our problems. It cannot set our goals. It cannot define our vision. Government cannot eliminate poverty or provide a bountiful econ-omy or reduce inflation, or save our cities, or cure illiteracy, or provide energy. And government cannot mandate goodness. . . . Those of us who govern can sometimes inspire. And we can identify needs and marshal resources. But we simply cannot be the managers of everything and everybody.

On one level, of course, President Carter had done nothing more than state ob-vious truths about the relation between government and the people. On another level, however, his declaration amounted to a repudiation of the New Deal's vision of governance. Certainly it was so understood by a substantial portion of his own party and helped fuel Edward Kennedy's insurgency against him.

The Democratic Party. Between 1961 and 1980, the Democratic Party had been transformed, institutionally and politically. As a result of the post-1968 changes in party rules, its governance structure shifted away from mediating institutions, such as state and local parties, and toward more direct forms of participation—from delegate selection through closed, hierarchical party structures toward reliance on primaries and caucuses. At the same time, power within the party began to shift away from relatively broadly based organizations, such as the AFL-CIO, and to-ward narrower advocacy groups organized around ethnicity, gender, or specific issue concerns. Reflecting this emerging group orientation, the party endorsed equal representation of men and women on all convention committees and called upon state parties to take "affirmative steps" to provide representation to women, minorities, and young people in "reasonable relationship" to their percentage of each state's population.[1]

Finally, the political base of the Democratic Party was changing. As late as 1960, the Republican presidential nominee was able to garner one third of the African American vote. By 1980, their support for Democrats was nearly unanimous. At the same time, reflecting broader changes in the economy, middle-class professionals were providing an increasing share of the party's total support. (It was the differences of outlook and interests between these professionals and the industrial working class that fueled the 1984 primary contest between Gary Hart and Walter Mondale.) Within organized labor itself, industrial unions, which tended to be white, male, and strongly anticommunist, were in decline, while public sector unions, which tended to be more diverse, female, and dovish, were gaining members and élan. Disaffected on racial, cultural, and religious issues, white southern Protestants deserted the party in droves, shifting the Democratic center of gravity toward the northern tier and the two coasts.

In key respects, the tale of Democratic Party transformation is one hand clapping, because the changes in the Republican Party were equally profound (and in some respects symmetrical). While Eisenhower split with Robert Taft by accepting the legacy of the New Deal, he agreed with Taft about the importance of government frugality and balanced budgets. Although the 1964 Goldwater insurgency did not affect an immediate takeover of the Republican Party, it energized a grassroots conservative movement that worked fervently for a smaller, less intrusive government. After a detour through Nixon's embrace of Keynesian fiscal policy and wage and price controls, by the end of the 1970s Republicans had become the party of tax cuts and supply-side economics. In foreign policy, the party shifted from détente to a confrontation with communism framed in quasi-Wilsonian terms. The entrance of large numbers of evangelicals and social conservatives moved the party toward the advocacy of "traditional values." As a result, the Republican political base shifted away from the Northeast, and to some extent the Midwest, toward the Sunbelt.

It is easy to forget how recently the Republican Party we now take for granted came into being. A glance at the party's 1972 platform is instructive. The opening section lays out a systematic effort to define and seize the political center, summarized in the following passage:

This year the choice is between moderate goals historically sought by both major parties and far-out goals of the far left. The contest is not between the two great parties Americans have known in previous years. For in this year 1972 the national Democratic Party has been seized by a radical clique who scorns our nation's past and would blight her future.

In foreign policy, the document highlights Nixon's trip to China, improved cooperation with the Soviet Union (including arms control treaties), and dozens of new international agreements. In addition to wage and price controls, the economic section of the platform featured initiatives such as tax reform tilted toward the middle class and the poor as well as a vigorous antitrust policy. The domestic policy section combined conservative positions on a handful of "backlash" issues (busing, welfare, crime, and drugs) with liberal stances on virtually everything else, including (among hundreds of items) affordable medical insurance, community mental health centers, increased spending for education and children's programs, and major urban mass transit legislation. The platform pointed with pride to the administration's path-breaking environmental record, including the creation of new executive branch agencies and the enactment of sweeping legislation addressing nearly every key environmental problem. The section on civil rights endorsed affirmative action, stepped-up federal enforcement of equal employment opportunity, voting representation in Congress for the District of Columbia, legislation and a constitutional amendment to lower the voting age, and ratification of the Equal Rights Amendment.

Notably, the 1972 Republican platform said nothing whatever about abortion. For that matter, neither did the Democratic platform. The abortion issue offers a case study of how an exogenous shock (in this instance, the *Roe v. Wade* decision) can over time force both parties to respond and change. The result was a symmetrical widening of the breach between the parties on what proved to be a defining issue.

In 1976, the Democrats said only that

> We fully recognize the religious and ethical nature of the concerns which many Americans have on the subject of abortion. We feel, however, that it is undesirable to attempt to amend the U.S. Constitution to overturn the Supreme Court decision in this area.

By 1980, while adopting roughly the same legal and policy stance, the Democrats' language was more supportive of the pro-choice position:

> We fully recognize the religious and ethical concerns which many Americans have about abortion. We also recognize the belief of many Americans that a

woman has a right to choose whether and when to have a child. The Democratic party supports the 1973 Supreme Court decision as the law of the land and opposes any constitutional amendment to restrict or overturn that decision.

By 1984, the party abandoned any verbal recognition of the concerns of abortion opponents and recast the issue in moral terms:

> The Democratic party recognizes reproductive freedom as a fundamental human right. We therefore oppose government interference in the reproductive freedom of Americans, especially government interference which denies poor Americans their right to privacy by funding or advocating one or a limited number of reproductive choices only.

A parallel-phase evolution occurred within the Republican Party. Although both the 1976 and 1980 platforms endorsed a constitutional amendment to reverse *Roe*, each acknowledged, at length, the diversity of legitimate views within the party. For example, the 1976 discussion began by declaring that

> The question of abortion is one of the most difficult and controversial of our time. It is undoubtedly a moral and personal issue but it also involves complex questions relating to medical science and criminal justice. There are those in our Party who favor complete support for the Supreme Court decision which permits abortion on demand. There are others who share sincere convictions that the Supreme Court's decision must be changed by a constitutional amendment prohibiting all abortions. Others have yet to take a position, or they have assumed a stance somewhere in between polar positions.

It was not until 1984 that the Republican Party, mirror-imaging the Democrats, expunged all reference to legitimate diversity within the party and recast the issue as a fundamental moral conflict about which compromise was unthinkable:

> The unborn child has a fundamental individual right to life which cannot be infringed. We therefore reaffirm our support for a human life amendment to the Constitution, and we endorse legislation to make clear that the Fourteenth Amendment's protections apply to unborn children. We oppose the use of public revenues for abortion and will eliminate funding for organizations which advocate or support abortions.

Similar stories could be told in several other areas. I would hazard the following generalization: the stark cultural cleavages we now take for granted as a defining (and in many ways disfiguring) feature of American politics represent choices that the parties made over time in response to external events. Whether these issues could have played out differently—that is, whether they could have become matters of argument within parties rather than warfare between them—is one of the imponderables of our recent political history.

DEFEAT AND DISMAY:
THE RISE OF THE NEW DEMOCRATS

The vicissitudes of the Democratic Party in the two decades between the election of John F. Kennedy and the defeat of Jimmy Carter sparked two waves of intra-party debate. Although the focus of this essay is the second of these waves, it is useful to begin by sketching the first.

The 1972 Democratic convention deeply traumatized key elements of the liberal coalition. "Cold War liberals," including many prominent northeastern intellectuals, had long supported a muscular anti-communist democratic internationalism, an activist state in economic and social policy, and a moderate form of moral traditionalism. In all these respects, Cold War liberals were comfortable with organized labor as led by George Meany and Lane Kirkland.

Most of these liberals had backed Lyndon Johnson's Great Society programs, including the War on Poverty. The setbacks these programs encountered, and the unexpected consequences they engendered, led many to question their faith in the power of activist government to remake society. These doubts, which helped catalyze the founding of an influential new journal (*The Public Interest*) constituted one of the key building blocks of what came to be known as neo-conservatism.

These liberals were also critical of the "counterculture." They believed in sobriety, moderation, self-restraint, respect for authority and the rule of law—indeed, in the panoply of bourgeois virtues. They rejected the counterculture's critique of these virtues, and they could not stomach the romantic antinomianism, much in evidence on the floor of the 1972 convention, with which the counterculture sought to replace them.

More than any other factor, however, it was foreign policy concerns that sparked the rise of neo-conservatism. As we have seen, the 1972 Democratic Party platform turned its back on a quarter century of liberal anti-communism. In an effort to turn back the tide, Cold War liberals clustered around the 1976 primary campaign of the quintessential liberal anti-communist, Sen. Henry (Scoop) Jackson. After Jackson's campaign failed, many invested their hopes in Jimmy Carter, who (although unconventional and virtually unclassifiable) was at least a southerner and former naval officer who might have been expected to resist the McGovernist thrust in foreign policy. Carter's failure to do so until he was surprised by the Soviet invasion of Afghanistan led many Cold War liberals to support the candidacy of Ronald Reagan. By the early

1980s, neo-conservatism was a spent force within the Democratic Party, although some Cold War liberals remained within the party and banded together in organizations such as the Coalition for a Democratic Majority, conducting an often lonely struggle to restore a lost consensus.

The neo-conservative exodus from the Democratic Party virtually coincided with the first stirrings of the New Democrat movement. As we will see, at the outset, New Democrats were less concerned with ideology than were the neo-conservatives and more concerned about the imperative of regaining a national majority. While sharing neo-conservatives' reservations about a McGovernist foreign policy, they cared more about domestic policy. Having come to political maturity after the Great Society, they were less seared by the alleged failure of activist government, less committed to retrenchment and more to reform. While offering a new moral basis for public policy, they did not feel besieged by the counterculture, which in any event had been watered down and domesticated. Finally, while offering a robust defense of what they termed "democratic capitalism," New Democrats were not as close to organized labor as many neo-conservatives had been. Indeed, New Democrats came to see unions as often creating narrowly self-interested obstacles to forward-looking policies and necessary reforms.

Walter Mondale's ill-fated presidential campaign brought discontent within the Democratic Party to a boil and helped spark the New Democratic movement. (Full disclosure: I served as Mondale's issues director throughout the campaign.) At the outset, Mondale hoped to run as the unifier of the Democratic Party, bridging its post-Vietnam internal divisions. But in response to the demands of the primary process and Gary Hart's surprisingly strong challenge, Mondale defined himself in ways that exacerbated fissures within the party over economic, foreign policy, and cultural issues.

This process continued throughout the general election as well. Mondale responded to President Reagan's supply-side budget deficits by running as a fiscal conservative. He responded to Reagan's aggressive defense and foreign policies by emphasizing cooperation with our allies and arms negotiations with the Soviets. He countered Reagan's embrace of conservative Protestant evangelicals by insisting on strict separation between church and state.

During the campaign, three overlapping but distinct sources of intra-party discontent and dissent emerged: Southern Democrats who were deeply troubled by the party's growing weakness in their region, a process that threatened statewide Democratic officeholders as well as members of the Congress; the staunchly anti-Soviet followers of Scoop Jackson who couldn't bring themselves to follow the neoconservatives into the Republican Party; and the so-called "Atari Democrats" who believed that a shift from an industrial to high-tech economy required new policies and institutional arrangements, including the diminution of the influence of organized labor within the Democratic Party. The concerns of these groups overlapped in complex ways. Hailing from a region with weak unions (and in many cases right-to-work laws), Southerners tended to sympathize with the Atari Democrats' skepticism about the relevance of New Deal-style labor organizations. A rising generation of progressive Southern governors understood that only new kinds of economic opportunities and increased investment in human capital could relieve their states' historic underdevelopment. Despite their differences with organized labor, they were also comfortable with the union-based Scoop Jackson Democrats' support for robust defense and foreign policies. And being forced to forge majorities in a region known for traditional cultural and social views, they were sensitive to the need to moderate the party's post-1972 tilt to the left on issues such as welfare, crime, and the role of religion in public life.

The institutional flagship of the New Democratic movement, the Democratic Leadership Council, opened for business in February 1985. Its early years, ably chronicled in Kenneth Baer's *Reinventing Democrats*, were given over to unsuccessful efforts to place the traditional party machinery and electoral rules in the service of more moderate voices within the party. As the 1988 election approached, the DLC helped engineer "Super Tuesday" (March 8, 1988) when Democrats in twenty mostly southern states were to go to the polls. The hope was that the more moderate southern voters would dilute the influence of Iowa and New Hampshire, forcing candidates toward the center and giving credible moderates a better chance of prevailing.

Events did not justify these hopes. To be sure, the New Democrats' young champion, Albert Gore Jr., prevailed in four southern states. But Jesse Jackson won five, while the eventual nominee, Michael Dukakis, carried off the biggest prizes—Florida and Texas. Super Tuesday demonstrated that Reagan had reconfigured southern politics by drawing conservative Democrats into the Republican Party, leaving southern Democrats with a coalition increasingly dominated by white liberals and African Americans. (This was especially the case during the primaries, which typically attract the more committed voters.) While the DLC's base among southern elected officials remained formidable, it became clear that a political strategy focused on the south would no longer suffice to rebuild a national majority.

Michael Dukakis's defeat in 1988 had a greater impact on the Democratic Party than did Walter Mondale's four years earlier. After all, Mondale had lost to one of the greatest political communicators of the 20th century, during a year in which the economy expanded robustly, the country was at peace, and the people could be persuaded that it was indeed "Morning in America." By mid-1984, few really expected Mondale to win; the question was whether his defeat would be respectable or (as it turned out) catastrophic. In contrast, by mid-1988 Dukakis had surged to a 17-point margin over George H. W. Bush. He was running as an able economic manager, the architect of the "Massachusetts miracle." The issue, he declared, was competence, not ideology. Nonetheless, the Bush campaign succeeded in portraying him as a liberal who was untested in defense and foreign policy while being out of touch with the social and cultural concerns of mainstream Americans. By September, Bush was in the lead.

In November, Dukakis lost not only white southerners, but also Catholics, moderates, independents, and voters in the heart of the middle class. His defeat threw the Democratic Party into near-crisis. According to traditional liberals close to organized labor, Dukakis lost because he had muted his differences with Republicans and had failed to offer voters a clear choice. There was nothing wrong with liberalism that full-throated advocacy couldn't cure. The DLC drew the opposite conclusion: Dukakis's defeat proved that contemporary liberalism, an amalgam of New Deal, Great Society, and McGovernite propositions and programs, had lost credibility and was no longer politically viable. The issue was ideology, not competence, but the ideology of the past could not serve as an effective counterweight to Reaganism. Nothing less than a new approach would do.

Having drawn this conclusion, the DLC abandoned its initial effort to play a meliorist, non-confrontational game within the party structure and went into open opposition. A key move was the founding of its own think tank, the Progressive Policy Institute (PPI), with the express aim of creating a new Democratic agenda and governing philosophy. In 1989, the DLC published a political and ideological manifesto, "The Politics of Evasion." (More full disclosure: I was its co-author, along with Elaine Kamarck.) The manifesto argued that Democrats had lost ground since the 1970s because the American people had come to see the party as inattentive to their economic interests, indifferent to their cultural concerns, and ineffective in defense of the country's interests abroad. To prevail, the next Democratic nominee would have to present himself as a wise steward of the people's resources, sympathetic to the cultural mainstream, and trustworthy as commander-in-chief. To nominate such a candidate, the party would have to set aside three entrenched myths: that it could forge a majority by mobilizing the few groups whose loyalty it still commanded; that it could win by nominating a more fervent liberal; and that it could continue to control the Congress despite repeated defeats at the presidential level. The manifesto buttressed these arguments with electoral, demographic, and survey data. It became the template for the thematic and policy development that largely occupied the DLC and PPI between 1989 and 1992.

The authors of the new progressive agenda worked out during those years understood it as an ensemble of innovative means to traditional progressive ends. On the domestic front, the dominant goal was to create an inclusive society unified around the principle of "equal opportunity for all, special privileges for none." In foreign policy, the guiding purpose was to foster, to the extent prudence permited, the worldwide spread of democracy. While this new progressive agenda called for, and required, a reformed but activist state, it broke with the statist progressivism of the early 20th century by arguing that a vigorous civil society and shared norms were needed as well to achieve historic progressive ends.

This is not to say that the new progressive agenda simply ratified the aims of contemporary liberalism. Indeed, it rested on three themes, each of which contrasted with contemporary liberalism as well as Reagan conservatism. *Equal opportunity* stood in opposition both to guarantees of equal outcomes and to pure Darwinian competition. Achieving equal opportunity required vigorous, well-targeted public policies, but it was up to individuals to take advantage of the opportunities made available to them. *Reciprocal responsibility* stood in opposition both to the philosophy of entitlement (getting without giving) and to pure individualism (you're on your own). Well-crafted public policies would bring together contributions and rewards. Finally, *community* stood in opposition both to rights-based individualism (the dominant ethos of modern liberalism) and to the cultural conservative ethos to promote moral behavior through state coercion. The ethic of community implied that as citizens we're all in this together and that one of the purposes of politics is to locate, and build upon, moral sentiments that we can freely share.

New Democrats framed these themes with an historical analogy. At the end of the 19th century, the transition from an agricultural to an industrial economy drove profound changes in American society and made necessary a new public philosophy and new approaches to economics, culture, political institutions, and foreign relations. The Progressives' response to these challenges, set forth in works such as Herbert Croly's *The Promise of American Life*, found early champions in political leaders such as Theodore Roosevelt and Hiram Johnson and reached full flower in Franklin Delano Roosevelt's New Deal. At the end of the 20th century, the United States was undergoing an equivalent transition, from the industrial to post-industrial economy, with equally profound consequences for our society and politics. The challenge for New Democrats was to understand the practical implications of these changes and to reflect them in innovative public policies.

Reflecting on these changes, New Democrats drew a number of conclusions that guided policy development. First, economic transition implied changes in the structure of opportunity. Individuals' economic prospects were likely to depend less on collective arrangements and more on their own individual training and skills. Second, changes in the basis of income and wealth implied shifts in the electorate. As the middle class came to be dominated by professionals and "knowledge workers," its outlook would change as well: the new middle class was likely to be less concerned with guaranteed security, and more interested in opportunity, choice, and rewards commensurate with their contributions. Third, markets would play a more central role in the new economy than in the old industrial economy, and the playing field would tilt against both industrial-era oligopolies and increasingly sclerotic public bureaucracies. This implied, in turn, the need for a reformed government that made more effective use of choice, market mechanisms, and new information technology.

These themes and broad propositions drove detailed policy development, of which I can present only the highlights.

To overcome Reagan-era budget deficits and set the stage for sustained economic growth, economic policy began with fiscal discipline, including cutting programs and closing corporate tax loopholes. Forward-looking features of economic policy included a focus on innovation and entrepreneurship, a new emphasis on education and training, and a range of mechanisms (which came to be known collectively as "democratic capitalism") for ensuring that workers in the new economy were able to obtain a fair share of its rewards. To address the problems of the working poor, New Democrats advocated a dramatic expansion of the Earned Income Tax Credit (EITC) rather than the industrial-era minimum wage. In another break with policies advocated by organized labor, New Democrats endorsed free trade treaties and steadily increasing global openness as the core of international economics.

In domestic policy, New Democrats developed policies based on three principles: using market mechanisms for progressive purposes; aligning programs with mainstream values; and reinforcing an ethic of reciprocity. Examples of the first included market-based health insurance and environmental regulation; of the second, welfare reform, 100,000 new police in local communities, and policies to shore up the two-parent family; of the third, a new program of national and community service that would offer full-time volunteers substantial post-service benefits to fund education and training.

In foreign policy, finally, New Democrats developed policies that put our diplomacy and armed forces in the service, not only of our interests, but also our ideals. The end of the Cold War did not mean the end of danger, but it did require new equipment, weapons systems, and training consistent with the changing mission of the U.S. military. The focus was not on cuts, as many liberals advocated, but rather on investments in reform. Overall, the emphasis was on "democratic internationalism"—comprehensive engagement abroad to promote democratization and deeper cooperation among democratic nations.

Bill Clinton's emergence as the New Democratic standard-bearer is an oft-told tale that I will not repeat here. Suffice it to say that he combined an intellectual mastery of policy detail with an intuitive flair for framing arguments to appeal to diverse constituencies, including traditional liberals. During the 1992 campaign, Ross Perot's surprising rise both reflected and gave new momentum to concerns about the budget deficit, creating a political predicate for New Democratic fiscal restraint. At the same time, the waning of the Cold War and rapid end to the first Gulf War reduced the salience of defense and foreign policy concerns, which were not Clinton's strong suit. The real pivot turned out to be values-laden domestic policy issues. Clinton convinced a key segment of the electorate that he was serious about breaking with Democrats' previous approaches to welfare and crime. The campaign's key TV spot, featured in swing states in the crucial two weeks before Election Day, went as follows:

> They're a new generation of Democrats, Bill Clinton and Al Gore. And they don't think the way the Old Democratic Party did. They've called for an end to welfare as we know it, so welfare can be a second chance, not a way of life. They've sent a strong signal to criminals by supporting the death penalty. And they've rejected the old tax-and-spend policies.

BILL CLINTON'S PRESIDENCY AND THE FUTURE OF THE NEW DEMOCRATIC MOVEMENT

Many analysts have observed that the first two years of the Clinton administration were a mixed bag for New Democrats and a disaster for the Democratic Party. I do not dissent from either of these judgments. Because the latter is so obviously true, let me focus on the former.

In economic policy, despite pitched battles within the White House and the party, Clinton stuck to New Democratic guns far more that most predicted. Early on, he rejected traditional fiscal stimulus in favor of restraint and deficit reduction. With a characteristic mix of persuasive public advocacy and one-on-one politics, he managed to move his controversial free trade agenda forward, getting both the North American Free Trade Agreement (NAFTA) and the latest round of General Agreement on Tariffs and Trade (GATT) through the Congress over staunch Democratic opposition.

Domestic policy presented a very different picture. In a shoot-out between traditional liberals and New Democrats, the president gave priority to health care over welfare reform, with disastrous results. While his crime bill did include substantial federal support for more police on the streets in lo-cal communities, the debate in Congress highlighted the issue of gun con-trol, a significant negative for many southern and rural Democratic mem-bers. Other high profile social issues included the unfortunate controversy over gays in the military, executive orders that adopted an uncompromising position on abortion, and a racial discussion dominated by the failed nomi-nation of Lani Guinier as Assistant Attorney General for Civil Rights.

In the area of governance and citizenship, things went better. Under the leadership of Vice President Gore, government reform and "reinvention" moved forward on a broad front. And presidential leadership was key to early passage of legislation restructuring and expanding opportunities for national and community service, though not as much as New Democrats had hoped.

Defense and foreign policy were far less successful, in part because Clin-ton's interests lay elsewhere during the early years, and also because senior administration leaders proved unable to forge a hard-edged consensus or (in some instances) even to manage their own agencies effectively. The results were a muddle in the Balkans, an embarrassing flip-flop on trade with China, and a fiasco in Somalia the reverberations of which extended far beyond the borders of that unfortunate country. Had these reverses not coincided with a period of low public concerns about foreign affairs, the political conse-quences might well have been quite serious.

In sum, then, the first two years of the Clinton presidency offered two clear wins for the New Democrats, one for traditional liberals, and one irrelevant draw. But the liberal victory occurred in domestic social policy, which was highly visible, intensely controversial, and largely unsuccessful. The presi-dent's New Democratic economic policies were slow to show gains, while the governance agenda had much less political salience. As a result, Clinton's profile was largely defined and judged in traditional liberal rather than re-formist New Democratic terms. The result was a rout in the 1994 elections, with Democrats losing control of both houses of Congress for the first time in more than forty years.

In several respects, Clinton fared better with the Republican-dominated Congress during his second two years. He managed to resist ill-judged and draconian budget cuts while laying the foundation for an eventual bipartisan balanced budget deal. And after blocking welfare bills he regarded as unbal-anced, he was able to redeem his campaign pledge to "end welfare as we know it." (His decision to sign the legislation highlighted continuing disputes between liberals and New Democrats and sparked several resignations from his administration.) As his economic policies took hold and growth shifted into a higher gear, public sentiment turned steadily in his direction, and he was able to win a comfortable victory over Bob Dole in the presidential election of 1996.

From a New Democratic perspective, however, the victory came at a price. Following the 1994 defeat, Clinton had turned to a controversial operative, Dick Morris, as his principal political advisor. Morris advocated and helped execute a strategy of what he called "triangulation" designed to lift the president above, and position him apart from, both political parties. The placement of a series of New Democratic proposals within this political frame helped tarnish the movement's agenda with the brush of political opportunism. This in turn fed the (mistaken) view that Clinton's acceptance of a balanced budget and welfare reform were the products of calculation rather than principle.

As a result, many liberal-leaning Democrats began characterizing the New Democratic agenda as not only wrong-headed, but also deeply cynical. In the aftermath of Clinton's budget deal with the Republicans in the summer of 1997, the House minority leader, Richard Gephardt, declared that the agreement represented not only "a deficit of fairness, a deficit of tax justice, and . . . a deficit of dollars" but also a "deficit of principle." In a December 1997 speech regarded as laying the foundation for an eventual presidential candidacy, Gephardt broadened his critique:

> New Democrats . . . [are those] who set their compass only off the direction of others—who talk about the political center, but fail to understand that if it is only defined by others, it lacks core values. And who too often market a political strategy masquerading as policy.

The final years of the Clinton administration represent a huge missed opportunity. Had it not been for the atmosphere of scandal and political conflict, exacerbating the already high level of partisan rancor, it might have been possible to take advantage of prosperity and the mounting budget surplus to address some long-deferred challenges and to place troubled entitlement programs on a sounder basis for the future. Instead, the administration made sporadic proposals (often in the annual State of the Union speeches) and then resorted to holding actions designed to ward off Republican tax cuts.

One especially unfortunate result of the lingering scandal was that the party's 2000 presidential nominee, Vice President Gore, felt compelled to distance himself from the president whom he had served so loyally and ably. In the process of effecting this separation, he deemphasized the very real achievements of the administration, many of which rested on New Democratic foundations, and resorted to a generic populist message that blurred the party's future.

CONCLUSION: THE NEW DEMOCRATIC
MOVEMENT AND THE FUTURE OF THE PARTY

As I draft this essay, shortly after the end of the 2004 primary season, the Democratic Party's future is still in doubt. Although deeply controversial within the party, the DLC's early intervention against Howard Dean (as a return to McGovernism) helped lay the foundation for his defeat. On the other hand, the only candidate to hew faithfully to the New Democratic creed, Joe Lieberman, failed to gain any traction whatever. Nor, interestingly, did the candidate backed by most of organized labor fare well. Dick Gephardt did miserably in Iowa, where industrial unions remain influential, and soon left the race. The winning candidate made himself generally acceptable to all the party's principal factions while clearly articulating the principles of none. In an atmosphere polarized by the policies of the Bush administration and rendered desperate by Republican control of all branches of government, Democrats were less interested than in years past in partisan wrangling and more concerned about maximizing their chances of victory.

Some divisive issues from the past are now off the table. Crime and welfare are not the burning controversies they were a decade ago. For better or worse, the party no longer debates abortion or affirmative action. And most party leaders have now accepted, some more grudgingly than others, the basic outlines of the Clinton formula for fiscal discipline.

Differences remain, of course. Trade emerged as the most divisive economic issue of the primary campaign, with the New Democrat position on the defensive. Even John Kerry, a longtime free trader, felt compelled to make protectionist noises, while John Edwards (a fresh face and able campaigner who enjoyed significant support among New Democrats) sounded like a senator from a state with a dying textile industry. On the foreign policy front, the war in Iraq reopened some of the party's Vietnam-era wounds. And here again, the New Democratic position came under pressure. Two of the three senators in the race who had voted for the Fall 2002 resolution authorizing President Bush to take action ended up opposing the $87 billion supplemental appropriation for troop support and Iraqi reconstruction. One cannot help suspecting that they would have supported it, absent the rigors of the primary campaign.[2]

Toward the beginning of this essay, I remarked that Bill Clinton won the presidency in 1992 on the basis of New Democratic ideas that enjoyed significant support in the country as a whole, but less support within his own party. Today, nearly twelve years later, less has changed than might have been expected. Bill Clinton failed to institutionalize his political success. Despite the DLC's energetic efforts, New Democrats have yet to become a real grassroots movement. They do constitute a growing network of state and local elected officials, but they are still a minority. New Democrats continue to supply the bulk of fresh proposals for the party. But they often win the battle of ideas, only to lose the war of votes.

The 2004 Democratic Party convention illustrated the problem. While the delegates obediently ratified the party's platform and cheered its nominees, surveys showed that they stood well to the left of the platform and the nominees' muscular acceptance speeches on domestic and foreign policy as well as on social issues. The party that John Kerry and John Edwards lead into battle is temporarily united, not around ideas, but in its burning desire to remove George W. Bush from the presidency.

If the Kerry/Edwards ticket prevails, we can expect early battles between traditional liberals and New Democrats. The presidential transition might well witness a replay of the November 1992–January 1993 struggle within the nascent Clinton administration between the advocates of increased domestic spending and the proponents of fiscal restraint. For example, the president-elect might have to make a choice between an immediate push for his massive health care proposal and his pledge to cut the deficit by half within four years.

On the other hand, if the Kerry/Edwards ticket goes down to defeat, the usual cycle of intra-party recriminations will resume as the pent-up energy and resentment of traditional liberals who held their peace in the name of victory bursts forth. The candidacy of Howard Dean showed where the hearts of the party's grassroots activists really lie, and it is difficult to believe that they would not find champions of their cause with presidential ambitions.

In short, while some of the issues that have divided traditional liberals and new Democrats since the 1980s have faded, others remain salient, and the war in Iraq has created passionate new cleavages. Whether the 2004 ticket wins or loses, it is safe to predict that this long-running struggle will resume.

NOTES

1. Jules Witcover, *Party of the People: A History of the Democrats* (New York: Random House, 2003), p. 574.

2. Senator Joseph Biden, a close advisor to Senator Kerry, has been quoted as saying that Kerry's decision not to support the $87 billion appropriation was "tactical," an effort to "prove to Dean's guys [that] I'm not a warmonger." See Philip Gourevitch, "Damage Control," *The New Yorker*, July 26, 2004, p. 55.

Chapter Two

Strategic Challenges Facing the Democratic Party (2004)

As I draft this essay in the summer of 2004, bad news from the Middle East dominates the airwaves and diverts attention from the modest economic improvements and from the bitter conflict over gay marriage that might have driven a peacetime election. George Bush has bet his presidency on success in Iraq, a gamble he may well lose. While the salience of defense and foreign policy issues is like to remain higher than during the brief interregnum between the collapse of Communism and the rise of Al Qaeda, support for military strategies based on preventive wars and Wilsonian hopes may fade. Given the facts on the ground, the public may come to view John Kerry's brand of cautious internationalism as prudent rather than indecisive.

However important these developments may be in the short term, the focus of this essay lies elsewhere. My principal interest lies in the slow-moving but massive changes in American society over the past generation that have reconfigured the fault-lines of American politics. Two of these changes—the impact of family structure and religion—are well known. To summarize: in the 2000 election, Albert Gore, Jr. did 10 percentage points better among unmarried men than married men, and 15 points better among unmarried than married women. Gore carried the 14 percent of voters who never go to church by 29 points over George W. Bush, while losing to Bush by 27 points among the 14 percent of voters who attend religious services more than once a week.

In this essay, I focus on the consequences of two less-discussed changes: the historic decision of the Democratic Party to become the party of civil rights, women's rights, and environmental protection; and fundamental shifts in the economy that have reconfigured the U.S. class structure. My thesis is that as a result of these shifts in political plate tectonics, today's Democratic Party is and will remain very different from the party of John F. Kennedy and

Lyndon Johnson. If a new progressive majority is to be built, it must be on terms other than those that sustained the Democratic Party from the New Deal to the Great Society. To see why, I begin with an analysis of two key political insurgencies since Johnson's decision to withdraw from the 1968 presidential contest.

A TALE OF TWO INSURGENCIES

In 1968, Hubert Humphrey received less than 43 percent of the popular vote, down 18 percentage points from Lyndon Johnson's 1964 landslide victory over Barry Goldwater. The 1968 winner, Richard Nixon, improved on Goldwater's showing by only 4 percentage points. The vast majority of Democratic defectors voted for George Wallace, who received 13.5 percent of the total. Within four years, the Republican Party had brought the Wallace voters into the fold. As a result, Republican candidates won four of the five presidential contests held in the 1970s and 1980s, with margins of victory averaging more than 14 percentage points. (The lone Democratic winner during these two decades prevailed by only 2 points.)

This era of Republican dominance came to an end in 1992, when George H. W. Bush, who had received nearly 54 percent of the popular vote in 1988, collapsed to only 38 percent. The winner, Bill Clinton, actually did 3 points worse than had Michael Dukakis in 1988. In the largest insurgency since 1912, Ross Perot received an astonishing 19 percent of the vote.

On taking office in 1993, President Clinton faced a political challenge similar to that of Richard Nixon in 1969. Cementing the bulk of the Perot voters into the Democratic Party would create a new era of reliable national Democratic majorities. This did not happen. Despite Clinton's success in eliminating the federal budget deficit, the economic issue Perot had emphasized, two-thirds of Perot's voters ultimately drifted back to the Republican Party, erasing Clinton's 5 point margin of victory over the first President Bush and creating a virtual tie in 2000.

Why did Democrats fail where Republicans had succeeded? The answer says much about the contours and dynamics of contemporary American politics.

When Perot ran for president a second time in 1996, he received only 8 percent of the vote. His hardcore supporters were predominantly white, male, lower income, and less educated, and they hailed from small-town and rural America. Up to the 1960s, many would have considered themselves conservative Democrats. But by the late 1990s that designation had become all but oxymoronic, as had "liberal Republican." (By the 2000 election, only 5 percent of the electorate considered themselves conservative Democrats, and only 2 percent liberal Republicans.) As a result, George W. Bush picked up the lion's share of the hardcore Perot voters, turning Clinton's 49-41 popular vote edge over Bob Dole into a 49-49 tie.

The exit polls tell the tale.

	2000		1996		
	Gore	Bush	Clinton	Dole	Perot
White men	36	60	38	49	11
HS grad only	48	49	51	35	13
$30-50K	49	48	48	40	10
Rural areas	37	59	44	46	10

In each of these demographic categories, George W. Bush's 2000 total was roughly the sum of the Dole and Perot votes in 1996.

The tenor of Al Gore's campaign renders these results all the more striking. To the dismay of his New Democratic supporters, Gore elected to wage the contest on the basis of a classic populist theme, "the people versus the powerful." The point was to focus the attention of downscale white voters on class and corporate privilege while de-emphasizing divisive cultural issues. This strategy was a dismal failure. As a leading analyst of American politics, Ruy Teixeira has observed that Gore lost white working class voters by 17 points; among white working class men, his margin of defeat was 34 points.

Gore did especially poorly among white Protestants, receiving only 34 percent of their vote, versus Bush's 63 percent. As political scientist Gerald Pomper has noted that by a margin of 25 points, secular voters were more likely to support Gore than were frequent churchgoers. In short: in the 2000 election cultural identity trumped economic class.

THE DEFECTION OF WHITE MALES

Race as a key component of cultural identity is an old story in American politics. Over the past generation, cultural identity has come to be defined partly in gender terms as well. Compare the two closest elections of the past three decades. In 1976, Jimmy Carter received 50 percent of the popular vote to Gerald Ford's 48 percent. There was no gender gap whatever; Carter's margin (50-48) was the same among men and women. In 2000, by contrast, Al Gore prevailed among women by eleven percentage points (54-43) while losing men to George Bush by the same margin (53-42). Gore fought Bush to a draw among white women while losing white men by 24 percentage points.

It is hardly an exaggeration to say that every major development of the past generation worked to push white men away from the Democratic Party. For some, the civil rights revolution was the trigger; for others, the rise of feminism and its institutionalization in the party's official structure. The rhetoric employed by high-profile extremists in these movements, who denounced white men as racist and patriarchal oppressors, exacerbated these effects. Conflict within the Democratic Party sparked by the events of 1968 led to rules changes that diminished the power of labor unions, for decades centers of white male political influence and social standing.

As Thomas Edsall has pointed out, the union movement itself has undergone fundamental changes during this period. After surging from 13 percent to 37 percent of the private sector workforce between 1930 and 1960, the union share of that workforce has collapse to just 8 percent today, the lowest level in a century. At the same time, the balance of power within the union movement has shifted toward the public sector: organized government workers have risen from only 17 percent of the union movement in 1976 to nearly half today. And men have declined from 83 percent of union members to under 60 percent today. The result of this transformation is that working class men in the private sector—the heart and soul of the electorate that narrowly made John F. Kennedy president—are now far more likely to be outside the influence of organized labor and to be exposed to a wider range of political and cultural forces that shape their outlook and their votes.

Developments in foreign and defense policy also played a role in pushing white men away from the Democratic Party. Democrats became the epicenter of opposition to the Vietnam War, a stance that spilled over into a broader critique of the Cold War defense budget and establishment, of assertive internationalism, and even of the United States. These developments offended many white men who were traditional patriots and favored a strong national defense. Gun control, which many white men saw as the translation of defense dovishness into domestic policy, made matters worse and helped cement Democrats' image as the party of weakness.

At the same time, the role of government shifted. As Anna Greenberg and others have pointed out, white males were the principal beneficiaries of New Deal policies. By contrast, Great Society programs largely aided women and minorities. And for two decades (1973–1993), the federal government failed to address the problem of wage stagnation, which hit less well-educated white men especially hard. Even the more successful economic strategy of the Clinton years—which improved the status of the working poor (through the Earned Income Tax Credit), minorities who found jobs for the first time in tight labor markets, and professionals who profited from the increased demand for their skills as well as the stock market surge—did relatively little for men in the heart of the middle class. By the 2000 presidential election, the majority of upscale white men came to believe that they needed nothing from government except to be left alone, while many downscale white men concluded that government either did not understand how to help them or did not care enough to do so. Because differing attitudes toward the role of government continue to define the left/right continuum in American politics, the rise of anti-government sentiment among white men produced a shift toward ideological conservatism. And because the major political parties have become more ideologically polarized, this shift in white male sentiment led inexorably to a move away from the Democrats.

A closer look at sentiments recorded in exit polls and post-election surveys adds precision to the understanding of white male flight from the Democratic Party in 2000.

As a group, white men were substantially more conservative than is the electorate as a whole. Only 16 percent identified themselves as liberal, versus 20 percent for the general electorate; by contrast, 35 percent regarded themselves as conservative (versus 29 percent overall).

Not surprisingly, only 19 percent of white men saw Gore as sharing their view of government (versus 30 percent for the electorate as a whole); while 43 percent saw Bush as sharing their view of government (34 percent for the electorate). Fifty-seven percent of white men saw Gore as too liberal on the issues; only 34 percent thought he was "about right." Conversely, 58 percent thought Bush was about right on the issues, while only 36 percent thought he was too conservative.

White men in 2000 displayed a distinctive outlook in three key issue areas: economics/role of government, defense/foreign policy, and social/cultural issues.

Economics/role of government. Only 32 percent of white men believed that government should do more, versus 45 percent of the electorate as a whole. White men gave a higher priority than did other voters to cutting federal income taxes and reducing the national debt, and a lower priority to Social Security and other domestic programs. A plurality of white men felt that the new president should cut taxes before doing anything else and were more supportive of across-the-board (rather than targeted) tax cuts than was the electorate as a whole. While a solid majority of the electorate was willing to consider investing a portion of payroll taxes in private Social Security accounts, white men supported this proposal by an overwhelming 66 to 34 margin.

Defense/foreign policy. White men were somewhat more likely than other voters to cite world affairs as the single issue that mattered most, and they were much more likely to believe that the U.S. military had gotten weaker during the past eight years. While the electorate as a whole had more confidence in Gore's ability to handle an international crisis than in Bush's, white men felt just the reverse.

Social/cultural issues. In some respects, the outlook of white men on social and cultural issues tracks that of the electorate as a whole. White men were no more likely than others to believe that the country was on the wrong track, morally speaking; that the president should be a moral leader as opposed to a government manager; or that abortion should be illegal in most or all circumstances. On the other hand, there was a huge gap between white men and others on the issue of guns. While 62 percent of the electorate supported stricter gun laws, that figure falls to 45 percent for white men. This gap played a significant role in the 2000 presidential election, when the share of voters from gun-owning households surged to 48 percent, versus 37 percent in 1996. A post-election survey by Stan Greenberg also found that other cultural issues—especially Gore's down-the-line support for abortion and perceived support for gay civil unions—helped drive white males toward Bush.

There is also evidence that white men were more likely than others to view the 2000 election through the prism of candidate character. Higher percentages of white men disapproved of Bill Clinton as a person; thought that the Clinton presidency would be remembered for scandals rather than policy accomplishments; felt that honesty was the quality that matters most in a president; and concluded that Gore was willing to "say anything" to get elected.

These cultural issues combined to shape the white male vote in 2000. For example, according to Greenberg, non college-educated white men under 50 regarded the rights of gun owners and the need to restore the military as the strongest reasons to vote for Bush. They voted against Gore because of concerns about his personal trustworthiness and his anti-gun position.

THE RISE OF THE PROFESSIONAL CLASS

The shrinkage of the middle class and widening gap between the wealthy and the poor are some of the most frequently discussed features of contemporary American life. Some see these developments as the basis for restoring a class-based politics by mobilizing lower-income groups in favor of a return to a more interventionist central government that buffers Americans against insecurity.

The tacit assumption behind this line of argument is that the income gap is growing because of downward mobility—that is, because a substantial portion of the population is being forced out of the middle class into working poverty. No doubt this is the case for some individuals. But in the aggregate, this assumption is false. At the end of the boom of the 1990s, the percentage of low-income families stood a bit below where it was in 1972, at the end of the post-war boom. The heart of the middle class is shrinking, not because poverty is on the march, but because millions of Americans are surging into the ranks of the upper middle-class and wealthy.

We can divide the economic history of the 20th century into three roughly equal phases. During the first third of the century, the U.S. economy moved from a system of agricultural production, craftsmen, and individual entrepreneurs to industrial mass production. By the end of that period, a newly mobilized industrial working class was becoming the driving force in American politics. During the second third of the century, the political accomplishments of the working class, coupled with America's post-war domination of the world economy, had produced a mass middle class and a politics shifting toward middle-class concerns. In the last third of the twentieth century, the shift toward a highly educated and professionalized post-industrial economy produced fundamental changes in modes of production and in the occupational structured. (By the end of the century, fully eight in ten Americans were engaged in the production of services and ideas, versus only three in ten at the beginning of the century.) In turn, this post-industrial transformation generated the first mass upper-middle class in human history. The consequences of the momentous shift in the U.S. class structure are still playing out.

In 1968, only 23 percent of the population earned $50,000 or more (in 1996 dollars). By 1996, their share surged to 34 percent. During that same period, the heart of the middle class (families earning $25,000 to $50,000 a year) declined from 39 percent to only 30 percent of the population. This trend is not the artifact of an arbitrary definition of the middle class: from 1968 to 1996, the percentage of American families earning in excess of $75,000 rose by almost ten points, from 6.8 to 16.4, while the percentage earning $25,000 to $75,000 declined by more than seven points.

Compared to the 1970s, the returns to education beyond high school roughly doubled in the 1980s and continue at high levels today. In 1976 a person with a post-graduate degree could earn on average 2.6 times as much as someone without a high school education; by the late 1990s a person with a post-graduate degree could earn, on average, 4 times as much as someone with no high school degree.

There is real anxiety for those who remain in the middle and bottom of the middle class and who see the upward mobility of others but not themselves.

There is a basis for their anxiety: a report by the Bureau of Labor Statistics (BLS) in the mid-1990s indicated that Americans in the middle—those making between ten and fifteen dollars per hour—had seen a decline in their real earnings during the previous decade. Indeed, between 1973 and 1999, median real hourly wages of workers with a high school degree declined by 11 percent, from $13.34 to only $11.83, and this trend is continuing. A recent BLS report, analyzed by the Progressive Policy Institute's Robert Atkinson, shows that between 1999 and 2002, jobs that pay middle-class wages grew more slowly that higher-paid knowledge jobs at the top and lower-paid service jobs at the bottom, while wages for occupations in the top quintile grew three to four times faster than those for working-class earners in the fourth quintile.

Long-term income shifts stemming from increases in the economic salience of education are having important consequences for our political life. One of the most stable findings in political science is the fact that more than any other single factor, education predisposes citizens to participate in politics and to vote. As the heart of the middle class shrinks and the upper-middle class expands, the upscale bias of the electorate—those who actually turn out to vote—has expanded out of proportion to what would be expected simply given the increased share of highly educated people in the population. An analysis I coauthored with Elaine C. Kamarck in 1998 showed while the percentage of Americans in the voting age population with college degrees had risen from 15 percent to 22 percent between 1980 and 1996, the percentage of college-educated voters had increased from 28 percent to 43 percent. During this same period, the percentage of voters with less than a high school education had fallen even more rapidly than has their share of the voting-age population.

The electoral consequences of this shift are accelerating. In the 2000 election, voters from families with incomes of $50,000 or more constituted 53 percent of the total, sharply up from 39 percent in 1996 (and only 32 percent in 1992). Voters with family incomes in excess of $75,000 were 28 percent of the total, up from 18 percent. And voters making more than $100,000 were 15 percent of the total, up from 9 percent. As Gerald Pomper has noted, these changes were far greater than were changes in income during this period.

These developments have affected Democrats even more than Republicans. Republican voters have always been wealthier than the population as a whole. But over the past two decades, the gap between Republicans and the general population has remained constant. Not so for Democrats. In 1976, the income of the median Democratic presidential voter was roughly equal the national median; today, the median Democratic voter is significantly above the national median.

These upscale trends are mirrored in the subset of voters who participate in presidential primaries. When Kamarck and I examined the twenty-seven states for which we had presidential exit polls in 1992, we found that, on average, 38 percent of the Democratic primary voters in those states had a college or post-graduate degree while only 20 percent of the voting age population in those states had a college or post-college degree. We also found that the largest decline in participation had occurred among members of the electorate lacking a high school degree. Over time, the historically low participation levels of these voters had decreased in all eleven states for which we possess continuous data—sometimes by as much as 50 percent.

Based on a traditional class analysis, one would have expected the shift toward a society and electorate dominated by upper middle-class professional to work in favor of the party that has historically championed upscale economic interests. But as John Judis and Ruy Teixeira argue in *The Emerging Democratic Majority*, the reality is more complex. For much of the twentieth century, professionals tended to identify with corporate managers and were among the most Republican of occupational groups. As late as 1960, they supported Richard Nixon over Kennedy by a margin of 61 to 38. By 1980, however, fully 15 percent of professionals supported John Anderson's blend of social liberalism and fiscal moderation. In part because of his critique of Ronald Reagan's budget deficits, Mondale got 45 percent of the professional vote, 4 points higher than his overall total. Dukakis, Clinton, and Gore have all won solid majorities of this growing sector: in the four most recent presidential elections, professionals have backed the Democratic nominee by an average margin of 52 to 40.

Judis and Teixeira propose two principal explanations for this shift. First, professionals came increasingly to prize non-market occupational values such as creativity and autonomy, which put them at odds with the imperatives of mainstream corporate life. Second, during their college years, many aspiring professionals are influenced by movements for civil rights, women's rights, the environment, and (during the 1960s and 1970s) by the anti-war movement as well. (We can only speculate about the impact of the controversy over Iraq on the next generation of professionals.)

PROFESSIONALS, THE WHITE WORKING CLASS, AND THE FUTURE OF THE DEMOCRATIC PARTY

At the beginning of this essay, I noted the paradox of Al Gore's general election campaign: a blunt populist appeal to the "people" against the "powerful" failed to rally the white working class to his side. But there is a flip side to this paradox: despite this appeal, Gore was more successful among up-scale professionals than was Bill Clinton, whose 1996 campaign all but expunged references to economic and social class. Gore did 3 points better than Clinton among voters making more than $75,000 and 5 points better among voters making more than $100,000. Clearly, a strong tide is pulling better educated, higher income voters toward the Democratic Party, at just the moment when an equally strong tide is pushing white working class voters away.

Judis and Teixeira offer a straightforward response to these conflicting trends. The key to a new Democratic majority, they suggest, lies in a new synthesis—in discovering a strategy that "retains support among the white working class, but also builds support among college-educated professionals." To do that, they optimistically argue, Democrats need not choose between a populist politics focused on working class resentment and a professional politics that emphasizes quality of life; they can do both.

Perhaps. To the extent that the flight of white men from the Democratic Party reflects the lingering effects of the civil rights and women's rights movements, there is little that Democrats can or should do to reverse the tide. Racial and gender equality are fundamental organizing principles of the contemporary Democratic Party and represent irreversible moral commitments. Nor is the party likely to change its core position on abortion, although it could do more to signal that it welcomes a range of views on this subject and could relax its intransigent opposition to what many moderate voters see as reasonable limits. The exclusion of pro-life Democrat Bob Casey from the convention podium in 1992 continues to rankle many voters who are only moderately opposed to abortion, as does the party's stance on "partial-birth" procedures.

It is clear that the dynamics of the primary campaign in 2000 led the eventual nominee toward stances on gun control and gay rights that did not serve him well among most white male voters in the general election. I fully supported the stance that Gore adopted on these issues. In retrospect, however, it is clear that these principled positions entailed significant political costs. If Democrats speak about gun control and gay rights in ways that imply that no decent and reasonable person could have a different view, voters who feel marginalized, even demonized, by this kind of rhetoric are bound to retaliate. The evidence so far suggests that John Kerry understands this, and that the advocacy groups that have pressured prior Democratic nominees to adopt purist stances are backing off to maximize Kerry's chances of victory in November.

In the aggregate, white men may be said to have a distinctive cultural outlook. Even more than most Americans, they prize independence, individual choice, and personal integrity and strength. Men gravitate toward candidates they see as having the courage to stand up against the odds, even against the majority—witness the strong white male support for Ross Perot and John Mc-Cain. White men care less about verbal facility and eloquence than they do about the reliability of words spoken. Gore's poor showing among the former supporters of Ross Perot and the disappointed supporters of John McCain substantially weakened his candidacy. And by defying conventional wisdom about the irrelevance of defense issues in the post-Cold War era, Bush parlayed his advocacy of a rebuilt military into a perception of firmness and strength that fortified his standing among white men. (Bush's firmness in the face of difficulties in Iraq has helped shore up his support among white men, even as it is eroding in other parts of the electorate.)

This is in part a matter of style—of plain-speaking and consistency. But substance matters as well. Perot and McCain demonstrated the power of muscular reform rhetoric linked to compelling issues. Kerry might well be able to appeal to both working class white men and upscale professionals by focusing on the next generation of reform issues—government operations, the tax code, and health care are plausible possibilities—and by articulating bold positions in forceful, commonsense terms.

In addition, Democrats should flesh out a policy agenda that speaks to the interests of the still-forgotten middle class. The economic changes of the past generation have greatly improved the income and wealth of the upper middle class, and public policies such as welfare reform and an expanded Earned Income Tax Credit have begun to address the problems of the poor and near poor. But while the rapid income gains of the second Clinton term were more broadly shared than at any time since the early 1970s, over the past two decades taken as a whole the heart of the middle class has continued to struggle under the burden of stagnant wages and incomes and the continued erosion of unionized employment, particularly in manufacturing—trends that have hit white men especially hard.

Reformist Democrats will not be able to sustain an economic agenda of competition, technological change, and globalization without dramatic and credible policies in areas such as job training and retraining, wage insurance, and benefits that continue through periods of unemployment. Despite recent concerns about the offshoring of high-tech jobs, professionals still may feel less in need of these policies than do working-class voters. Democratic leaders must frame a case that gives professionals a material as well as moral stake in the future of working-class Americans.

All this said, however, for the foreseeable future Democrats cannot hope to regain the position among white working-class men they enjoyed in 1960, or even 1976, any more than Republicans can regain their standing as the party of Abraham Lincoln (or even Richard Nixon) among African Americans. While more nuanced stances on hot-button cultural issues may help, particularly when combined with progressive New Democrat positions on the role of government and the economic prospects of the middle class, Democrats cannot hope to compete on equal terms in small towns and rural areas. There is no principled and practical way of stemming the flight of Zell Miller and the people he represents from the Democratic Party.

There is a reason why the Democratic Party split so badly after 1968, and why the best thinkers and most skillful politicians have had such a hard time reunifying it. A new Democratic majority requires a coalition between upscale professionals and average workers. The problem is that these two groups do not understand their interests or their values in the same way. The upper middle class does not feel as vulnerable as do lower middle class workers and focuses more on "postmaterial" issues. In comparison with working class voters, professionals typically care less about economically activist government and more about fiscal discipline; less about trade protection and more about global markets; less about job loss and more about the environment; less about security and more about opportunity; less about authority and traditional values, and more about self-expression and inclusion.

These are distinctions that make a difference. For example, West Virginia has long been one of the most reliably Democratic, working-class states in national elections. In 1992, Bill Clinton won 48 percent of the West Virginia vote (about 58 percent of the major party vote), and in 1996 he won 52 percent (slightly more than 58 percent of the major party vote). In 2000, however, the Bush campaign parlayed working-class resentments over trade, environmental regulation, energy policy, and cultural issues into a stunning 53-47 victory over Gore.

As many political analysts have observed, a political party in a two-party system inevitably represents a diverse coalition, not a full consensus on policy or ideology. And coalitions can practice distributive politics, giving each of their major constituent groups something about which they deeply care. But while parties can give different things to different groups, they cannot give contradictory things to those groups. When Bill Clinton assumed office in 1993, he was forced to choose between a policy of fiscal moderation that appealed to moderates and a policy of public investment backed by unions and other key interest groups. He chose the former, rightly in my judgment. But he paid a huge price, with the congressional wing of his party during the first two years of his presidency, and then with the electorate in November of 1994. Similarly, he was forced to choose between leading off his domestic policy with comprehensive health care reform, as many traditional liberals were urging, or with welfare reform, as his New Democratic backers recommended. This time he opted to follow the liberals' advice, again with negative results for the party and with the electorate.

To hold a coalition together despite its internal differences, its members must agree on something that is at least as important to them as are the matters about which they disagree. A shared quest for political power is not enough. For an extended period, the commitment to tax cuts was enough to unite the otherwise fractious Republican coalition. No such unifying issue for Democrats has yet emerged. The deep antipathy most Democrats feel for President Bush and his principal advisors is generating a temporary suspension of internecine warfare and may be enough to yield victory in November. But then suppressed differences are likely to emerge.

For example, the Democratic Party is now divided between a peace faction and what the Progressive Policy Institute's Will Marshall has called "Blair Democrats." The moderate internationalists gathered around Kerry seem determined to see an amended version of the Iraq occupation through to a successful conclusion. This position, however, enjoys the support of a small and shrinking minority of Democrats and may prove unsustainable if instability continues and costs and losses mount.

Another example: the centerpiece of Kerry's domestic agenda is a major overhaul of the nation's health care and health insurance, estimated to cost between $600 and $900 billion over the next decade. But he has also endorsed a fiscal policy along the lines of the deficit-reducing restraint Clinton chose in preference to major new public investments. (Indeed, the complex and unpopular architecture of the Clinton health care plan was designed to avoid new burdens on the federal budget.) It does not require prophetic inspiration to foresee a clash between health care and fiscal moderation early in a Kerry administration.

The New Deal represented a coalition of have-nots, each part of which had something important to gain from activist government. While today's Democrats are united in rejecting laissez-faire, they do not agree affirmatively about the role of government, in part because their interests diverge. Low-wage workers have a direct stake in policies that boost their incomes. Public sector workers favor policies that maximize their job security, a stance that led Democrats into a political cul de sac during the 2002 debate over creating a department of homeland security. Urban and minority voters often want policies that increase opportunities for their children, even when these policies (school vouchers, for example) bring them into conflict with teachers' unions. Professionals want government policies that promote long-term economic growth and maximize scope for the kind of innovation in which they excel, even when these policies restrict public investment and increase insecurity for trade-sensitive sectors of the economy.

If Democrats are to become a stable governing majority once again, the synthesis analysts such as Judis and Teixeira recommend is surely necessary, and the "progressive centrism" they advocate is surely the beginning of wisdom. But speaking as someone who has labored with others of like mind for fifteen years to help make progressive centrism the heart of a new majority, I must admit that the terms of a synthesis that is politically as well as intellectually viable are not yet clear. Bill Clinton campaigned, and won, and sought to govern, on the basis of a program many elements of which enjoyed more support in the country than in his own party. Despite the efforts of Democratic leaders, and the undeniable successes of the Clinton presidency, party renewal remains a work in progress.

Chapter Three

Two Postmortems: The 2004 Elections and the Future of the Democratic Party (2005)

BROAD CONTOURS AND IMPLICATION OF THE DEMOCRATS' DEFEAT

There are two kinds of defeats in electoral politics. Some are expected, even felt to be inevitable (for example, Walter Mondale in 1984). Such losses are sad for the losers, but they do not lead the losing party to reflect on fundamentals. Other defeats are stinging because they are unexpected (for example, Michael Dukakis in 1988). In such circumstances, the defeated party believes that its candidate, agenda, and electoral strategy are clearly superior to that of the winner; the defeat experienced is not only surprising, but in a deeper sense unjust. This kind of defeat typically sparks self-reflection on the party's very identity. The presidential election of 2004 is more like 1988 than 1984 and is already producing among Democrats the willingness to reexamine fundamental premises.

It is essential to conduct this reassessment without recriminations, and with due regard to history. In the first place, there has been a conservative (or at least non-liberal) majority in U.S. presidential elections since 1968. In the 10 elections since Lyndon Johnson's 1964 landslide, the Republican candidates have averaged nearly 50 percent of the popular vote; Democrats, just 45 percent. During this period, the Democratic nominee has attained a majority of the popular vote only once (Jimmy Carter, and just barely, in 1976), while the Republican nominee has done so on five occasions (1972, 1980, 1984, 1988, 2004). In this long conservative cycle, Republican nominees begin with a structural advantage; it is remarkable when they lose, not when they win. And when Democrats do win, they are forced to function within, and adjust to, a hostile political environment. (In this regard, there are some intriguing parallels between Bill Clinton's presidency and the eight Eisenhower years that interrupted but did not terminate the New Deal hegemony.)

The 2004 presidential election may be regarded as the culmination of a 40-year cycle set in motion by the 1964 Civil Rights Act. Nearly all vestiges of the once-powerful Southern Democracy have been swept away, leaving only safe (mainly minority) House seats and a handful of southern senators. (Indeed, in the wake of Tom Daschle's defeat, all "Red State" Democratic senators, outside as well as within the South, should be placed on the endangered species list.)

This election also occurred within an even longer 50-year cycle of bold court decisions and popular reaction to them: on school desegregation in 1954, school prayer in 1962, abortion in 1973, and most recently, the constitutionalization of gay marriage by the Massachusetts Supreme Court. In part as a result of these decisions, a new traditionalist entente has emerged, submerging ancient interfaith enmities while uniting conservative Catholics, fundamentalist Protestants, and Orthodox against liberals and modernists in their respective denominations.

Let me now turn from history to the present. The 2004 election was notable is several respects. First, there was a huge mobilization of the electorate. Overall participation rose nearly 15 percent, from 105 million voters in 2000 to an estimated 120 million in 2004, yielding the highest turnout rate since 1968. In many key battleground states, participation rose even more: by 20 percent in Ohio, for example, and nearly 23 percent in Florida.

This massive mobilization was asymmetrical. The Democrat vote total rose from 51 to a record of more than 57 million, more than enough to assure victory in most years. But 2004 was not a normal year: the Republican total surged from 50.5 million to nearly 61 million, replacing George Bush's half-million vote deficit in 2000 with a healthy edge of about three and one-half million.

As the electorate grew, its ideological contours changed: while self-identified liberals as a share of the electorate remained roughly constant at 20-21 percent, the conservative share rose by about 4 percentage points, to between 33 and 34 percent. Of the 10 million new Republican votes, at least 7 million came from individuals who regard themselves as conservative, moving the median Republican voter to the right. Because moderates declined from 49 to 45 percent, the electorate became more polarized.

George Bush scored broad gains across the electorate. His share of the vote rose by 5 points among white women, by 7 points among Hispanics, 4 points among Catholics, 6 points among voters 60 years of age or older, 10 points among Americans with less than a high school education, and 11 points in large urban areas. He made no gains among college graduates and actually lost ground among highly educated professionals and young adults. (Contrary to early and erroneous press reports, voting by 18- to 29-year-olds surged this year by more than 4.5 million this year, and their participation rate rose by an amazing 9 percentage points.)

Elections are more than tactical and organizational exercises, of course; they are also (perhaps mainly) efforts of public persuasion. In this respect, one must conclude that the challenger's effort to build a compelling case against to incumbent was for the most part a failure. John Kerry did not succeed in persuading the American people that the decision to go to war in Iraq was a mistake or a diversion from the war on terror; that he could do a better job of either conducting that war or managing the economy; or that he would be a stronger and more effective leader. Despite numerous pre-election surveys to the contrary, in the end a solid majority of the electorate expressed their approval of President Bush's job performance. The President's victory was substantive as well as personal.

With sizeable gains in the Senate, and Democrats looking at 17 Senate seats they must defend in 2006, Republicans are in control of every branch of the national government, and a triumphant president is in control of the Republican Party. George Bush has the initiative; the question is what he will do with it. Early signs, particularly his post-election news conference and rare public statement by the acknowledged "architect" of his victory, Karl Rove, suggest that the next four years will be much like the past four years. President Bush will press a bold agenda that reflects conservative Republican principles, and he will consult and compromise with the opposition only to the extent necessary to move a partisan agenda through the Congress. In areas ranging from tax reform and Social Security privatization to drilling for oil in Alaska, changes in tort laws, and judicial nominees, bitter partisan controversy is likely to prove the norm.

With regard to foreign policy, Mr. Bush no doubt feels that he has gained a free hand to conduct the war in Iraq more or less as he wishes. It is doubtful that congressional Democrats will stand in his way, even if, as expected, he soon requests a massive supplemental appropriation ($70 billion is the current guess) to finance military operations. The war is the president's to end on the terms he regards as most consistent with the national interest. It remains to be seen, however, whether he will be able to deal with other foreign hotspots, from Iran and North Korea to the Israeli/Palestinian dispute, as long as the bulk of our land forces remain pinned down in Iraq and our international standing remains at such a low ebb.

So where do the Democrats go from here? To begin, the party is badly divided on national security. Some Democrats support the president's policies and endorse his worldview; others criticize those policies on grounds of prudence or execution; still others view them as wrong in principle. John Kerry's approach to Iraq, which created the appearance of indecision, reflected these splits without resolving them. While the next Democratic nominee may challenge the Bush foreign policy, the critique must be seen as resting on a clear and credible alternative.

Nor can the party stand pat on large economic issues. While Kerry's criticisms of the administration's budget deficit, trade deficit, and tax cuts had substantive merit, the Democratic nominee failed to persuade a majority that his alternatives were likely to work better. The American people are worried that the integration of 2.5 billion Chinese and Indians into world markets poses challenges for the U.S. economy that the policies of the 1990s do not suffice to address. Democrats urgently need a new narrative of success in the global marketplace—a compelling vision and sensible policies that offer average Americans more opportunity and security than they now enjoy.

And finally, the moral issues, over which so much ink has been spilled in recent weeks. Democrats cannot hope to compete for the right-wing Christian vote, and they should not try. But in the 2004 election, Democrats' largest losses came among less fervent believers—the broad mainstream of families worried about the erosion of moral standards and the corrosion of our culture. To address their concerns, Democrats will have to distance themselves from Hollywood, reduce their reliance on the judiciary as the engine of social change, and temper what appears to many to be intransigence on morally fraught policies. The modern Democratic Party will never turn its back on *Roe v. Wade*, but many Democrats quietly wonder why the party is falling on its sword over partial birth abortion. No doubt purists will reject policies built on such doubts as pandering or worse, much as they criticized Bill Clinton's approach to welfare in the 1990s. But history suggests that mainstream social policies work, and that proposing them opens up the possibility of renewed dialogue with a portion of the mainstream electorate that is no longer listening to what Democrats are saying.

MORAL VALUES AND RELIGION
IN AMERICAN POLITICS

In just a few months since the 2004 election, the "moral values" debate has already proceeded through two distinct phases. The much-maligned National Election Pool exit poll triggered the first: when voters were asked to pick, from a list of seven possibilities, the one issue that mattered the most in deciding how to vote, 22 percent chose moral values, compared to 20 percent for the economy, 19 percent for terrorism, and 15 percent for Iraq. Many people found this result startling, in part because so much of the campaign's public debate had revolved around the challenge of combating terrorism and the controversy over the war in Iraq. (The result seemed especially surprising because the conventional wisdom among political scientists and pollsters, strongly supported by recent history, is that cultural/moral issues come to the fore only when burning economic or foreign policy issues are absent.) The airwaves and op-ed pages soon filled with pundits deploring (or less frequently, applauding) what seemed to be a widening cultural/religious divide between progressives and traditionalists. Many urged Democratic leaders to pay less attention to tofu-eating Vermonters and more to the salt-of-the-earth folks who attend NASCAR races.

Rarely was an interpretation of a national election erected on such a slender empirical foundation, and a reaction soon set in. Citing a potential for "deep distortion," the polling director for ABC News revealed that he had argued in vain against including moral values as an option. Pollsters noted that different ways of posing questions about the impact of moral values on voting decisions yielded dramatically different results; not surprisingly, because voters disagreed about the meaning of the phrase. And besides, they argued, there was no compelling evidence that values issues had played a larger role in 2004 than in previous elections. The 2000 exit poll had included no comparable option, and a 1996 question about "family values" had yielded responses not vastly different from 2004. An *LA Times* exit poll suggested that the share of the electorate influenced by moral values was no higher in 2004 than in 1996, and only slightly higher than in 2000. The chief executive officer of America Coming Together, a "527" committee organizing get-out-the-vote efforts for Democrats, noted that in Ohio, the share of the electorate attending church regularly actually declined from 45 percent in 2000 to 40 percent in 2004. Political scientists found no convincing evidence that anti-gay marriage initiatives had raised turnout in the eleven states where they appeared on the ballot. On December 5, the *Washington Post* saw fit to publish an article on the front page of its highly regarded Outlook section with the heading, "The Anatomy of a Myth." And that, it seemed, was that.

Or maybe not. I want to suggest that when we probe beneath statistical aggregates to study specific population groups, and when we place this year's results in a broader historical context, we do after all find reasons to believe that "values" issues were unusually influential in the 2004 presidential election.

To get some perspective on this controversy, let me begin by distinguishing between long-term trends and the specifics of the 2004 election. Some scholars, such as political scientist Morris Fiorina and sociologist Alan Wolfe, reject the thesis that the American people have become more polarized along moral and ideological lines during the past generation. In one sense they are right: the majority of the people remain clustered around the mainstream rather than the extremes. But while the shape of public opinion has remained relatively stable, its distribution between the major political parties has not. As recently as the 1960s, the Democratic Party included substantial numbers of people who regarded themselves as conservatives. As recently as 1976, the Democratic presidential nominee enjoyed an edge among white born-again Christians. But over the past four decades, the political parties have become more internally homogeneous, while the gap between them has widened. In 1976, for example, 29 percent of conservatives supported Jimmy Carter; in 2004, only 15 percent of conservatives supported John Kerry. Twenty-six percent of liberals supported Gerald Ford in 1976; only 13 percent supported George Bush in 2004. During this period, levels of religious observance became key determinants of ideological self-identification and partisan affiliation. Today, 54 percent of Americans who attend religious services once a week or more consider themselves conservatives, versus only 26 of those who never attend. Sixty percent of frequent attendees voted for George Bush over John Kerry, versus only 34 percent of non-attendees.

While we don't know precisely what "moral values" meant to the voters who selected this phrase as the principal determinant of their vote, we can draw some inferences from what we know about these voters. They tend to be white, male, and married. Forty-two percent are white born-again Christians, twice the born-again share of the overall electorate. Fifty-seven percent regard themselves as conservative, and 59 percent as Republicans, versus 34 percent and 37 percent, respectively, for the electorate as a whole. twenty-three percent said that they valued a candidate's strong religious faith more than any other personal characteristic, compared to only 8 percent for the broader electorate. Eight in 10 of these voters supported President Bush over Senator Kerry.

We can also learn from a survey that the Pew Research Center for the People and the Press conducted in the days immediately after the election. When presented with a list of options, 27 percent of respondents choose moral values as the principal determinant of their vote. When offered an open-ended, unprompted question, only 14 percent of respondents volunteered some version of moral values—far less than in the alternative formulation, but still second only to Iraq. Within this broad category, some voters cited the general concept of sound morality; others specified social issues such as abortion and gay marriage, while a third group emphasized the personal morality of the candidate. When offered the first version of the question, 44 percent of the Bush voters chose moral values as the most important reason for their vote, versus only 7 percent of Kerry supporters. In responding to the second (unprompted) version of the question, a remarkable 27 percent of Bush voters volunteered moral values, as opposed to only 2 percent of Kerry supporters.

Ever since Karl Rove's famous lament about the 4 million missing evangelical votes in 2000, political commentators have been fixated on the Bush administration's outreach to this group. The exit polls suggested that these efforts achieved at least moderate success. Overall, the president raised his share of the white Protestant vote from 63 percent in 2000 to 67 percent in 2004. About half of these voters identified themselves as evangelical or born-again, up from 2000, although differences in exit poll categories made it difficult to determine the extent of the increase. The University of Akron's John Green, one of the leading researchers on politics and religion, notes that the president's share of the evangelical vote rose from 72 percent in 2000 to 78 percent this year, and that most of these gains came among evangelicals who reported attending church less than once a week. By contrast, Bush's share of the mainstream Protestant vote appears to have fallen slightly, from 56 percent to 52 percent.

Although political pundits focused more on conservative Protestants than on Catholics, a plausible case can be made that the Catholic vote contributed at least as much to the president's victory. A survey taken in July showed a dead heat (40-40) between Bush and Kerry among Catholics, with 18 percent undecided. In the end, however, the President raised his share of the Catholic vote from 47 percent in 2004 to 52 percent in 2004. In Ohio, where the Bush campaign sent large numbers of field workers to Catholic churches, the president received 55 percent of the Catholic vote, up from about 50 percent in 2000. John Green calculates that this shift netted Bush 172,000 votes, more than his eventual margin of victory in that state. In Florida, where the Catholic share of the total vote rose from 26 to 28 percent, Bush's share of the Catholic vote rose from 54 percent in 2000 to 57 percent in 2004. In combination, these shifts represented an additional 400,000 votes, roughly the President's Florida margin of victory.

What happened? One popular explanation is the strong intervention of some bishops against pro-choice Catholic candidates such as John Kerry, but the evidence does not support this hypothesis. Only 20 percent of Catholics supported denying communion to pro-choice Catholic politicians; only 16 percent felt that these politicians had an obligation to vote the way the bishops recommend; only 7 percent thought that the views of the bishops would have a significant impact on the way they themselves voted.

There is evidence, however, that another moral values issue—gay marriage—may have moved substantial numbers of Catholic voters toward the president. The mid-summer survey showed that fully 23 percent of Catholics "strongly" disapproved of making gay marriage legal and would definitely vote against a candidate they disagreed with on that issue, versus only 4 percent who strongly approved and were prepared to vote on the basis of that conviction. While President Bush voiced full-throated opposition to gay marriage, breaking with his own vice president to advocate a constitutional amendment banning the practice, John Kerry offered a more nuanced position, opposing gay marriage but favoring leaving the matter to the states. To the extent that Catholics interpreted Kerry's position as covert support for local gay marriage initiatives, this issue could well have moved some of them to support Mr. Bush.

To be sure, the exit polls do not allow us to say with confidence why Catholics shifted toward the President. But we do know that the Bush campaign worked very hard to win their support. According the Steven Waldman and John Green, the campaign appointed 50,000 local Catholic "team leaders." The President made a highly publicized trip in June of 2004 to visit the Pope, whose picture was then displayed on the campaign's website under the heading "Catholics for Bush." Meanwhile, pro-life groups ran ads blasting John Kerry for allegedly supporting abortion "in all nine months of pregnancy." It is hard to believe that these efforts did not have a measurable impact on Catholic swing voters.

The Bush campaign scored one of its more significant successes among Hispanic voters. While the polls remain in dispute, it is clear that the president increased his share of the Hispanic vote from 35 percent in 2000 to between 40 and 44 percent this year. One plausible explanation: increasing numbers of Hispanics are evangelicals rather than Catholics, and 60 percent of Hispanic evangelicals voted for Mr. Bush. Among Hispanic Catholics, Bush raised his support from 31 percent in 2000 to 42 percent this year. Based on a survey taken the day after the election, the veteran Democratic pollster Stanley Greenberg concluded that Republican appeals based on moral values accounted for much of the movement away from the Democratic nominee among Hispanics.

A similar dynamic appears to have been at work among African Americans. The president received 16 percent of the black Protestant vote, up from 9 percent in 2000, and black Protestants who attend church more than once a week gave Mr. Bush 22 percent of their vote. Interviews with black ministers suggest that Republicans were making inroads among black religious leaders with appeals to biblical teachings on issues such as gay marriage and abortion.

Another suggestive piece of evidence emerges from a survey of college students sponsored by the Center for Information and Research on Civic Learning and Engagement (CIRCLE). Although these students were notably more liberal and pro-Kerry than other age groups, fully 26 percent selected moral issues as the principal determinant of their vote. They did so in spite of the fact that the poll question specified abortion and gay marriage as instances of moral issues, which might well have narrowed the appeal of this option. Sixty percent of these respondents supported George Bush.

While the evidence suggests that questions of sexual conduct influenced voters' understanding of moral values, there are also indications that for many, the issue was much broader. In the aftermath of the election, *Washington Post* reporter David Finkel interviewed white evangelical voters in the small town of Sheffield, Ohio. The Leslie family had seen its annual income drop from $55,000 in 2001 to $35,000 this year. It didn't affect their vote: it wasn't President's Bush's fault; and besides, it wasn't the most important thing in life. "Jobs will come and go," said Cary Leslie, "but your character — you have to hang on to that. It's what you're defined by." And as far as they were concerned, it's what defined the President. "To know that he prays," said his wife Tara Leslie, "and I really believe he does — that's a huge thing." Cary summed up his interpretation of the election in a simple sentence: "It's a victory for people like us." It's difficult to imagine a more pointed depiction of the politics of identity.

In the fevered atmosphere of 2004, the politics of identity extended beyond debates over abortion and gay marriage, and even beyond religious affiliation and observance, to encompass issues of national security. President Bush succeeded in transforming the war in Iraq and the fight against terrorism into questions of basic values and American national identity. Earlier this year, the University of Virginia's Center on Religion and Democracy conducted a survey probing public attitudes towards America's role in the world. The Center found that while most Americans see our country as a force for good in the world, a significant minority does not. These dissenters are not evenly distributed between the political parties: 30 percent of Democrats are highly critical of America's global role, versus only 9 percent of Republicans. And religion reinforces partisanship: Americans who said that their religious beliefs were "not at all important" to them, most of whom are Democrats, were much more hostile toward America's role in the world than were those who religious beliefs mattered. Of these critics, the survey's author concluded that "they differ sharply [from the majority] in certain universal judgments. To wit, their hope for the future is for a world of diminishing emphasis on country, globalized standards of living, and flexible moral commitments grounded in secular truths. In their lack of a strong national identity and their secularism, they share more in common with many Europeans than with the majority of their fellow citizens."

In retrospect, this may have been the deepest "moral values" issue at stake in the 2004 election. While Republicans stood united in their belief in American exceptionalism, Democrats were badly divided, as they have been since Vietnam. President Bush was able to rally his party by sounding the trumpet of American virtue on the global stage. By contrast, John Kerry struggled to bridge the gap between Tony Blair Democrats, who agreed with the President's principles but deplored his inept policies, and Michael Moore Democrats, who rejected, root and branch, the idea of a global fight against terrorism and for democracy.

As we learned in Vietnam, the moral dimension of foreign policy cannot prevail indefinitely against facts on the ground. Eventually, the efficacy of means trumps the nobility of ends. If the President brings our occupation of Iraq to a successful conclusion, the Bush doctrine may well define a new values-based internationalism for some time to come. If so, this will reinforce the structural political advantage of the party that more fully embraces American exceptionalism. If not, the post-Vietnam understanding of limits to American power will likely rise from the ashes of Fallujah, once again redrawing the moral fault-lines of American politics.

Chapter Four

The Art of Association in Free Societies: Alexis De Tocqueville and Liberal Democracy (2000)

The past two decades have witnessed an explosion of interest in "civil society" on the part of both scholars and political activists. There are four principal reasons for this development. In the first place, events in the former Soviet bloc nations of central Europe dramatized the ways in which civil associations—labor unions, networks of dissident intellectuals, and churches, among others—could serve as effective sources of resistance to oppressive governments.

Second, "non-governmental organizations" emerged throughout the world as arenas for the emergence of previously unheard voices addressing issues of transnational significance such as the environment, population and consumption, the status of women, human rights, and even disarmament. (Witness the Rio, Cairo, and Beijing conferences, the anti-land mine treaty, and the influence of Amnesty International.)

Third, the concept of civil society—a realm of nonprivatized collective action that is voluntary rather than coerced and persuasive rather than coercive—constituted the basis for criticizing the excesses of both the state and the market. Liberals sobered by the limits of centralized governmental action began looking to voluntary associations as alternatives ways of fostering civic engagement and promoting public purposes. Conservatives troubled by the amoralism of the market and by its corrosive effects on social institutions turned toward voluntary associations as sources of stability and virtue. (Remarkably, the leading contenders for the year 2000 Democratic and Republican presidential nominations in the United States have both endorsed an expanded role for voluntary associations—including faith-based institutions—as partners with government.)

Finally, civil society speaks to the anxiety throughout the advanced industrialized world (and especially powerful in the United States) that traditional sources of socialization, solidarity, and active citizenship have become dangerously weak. Robert Putnam's "Bowling Alone," published in these pages five years ago, touched precisely this nerve of concern, sparking a conceptual, empirical, and political debate that rages unabated today.[1]

Not surprisingly, this upsurge of interest in voluntary associations has coincided with renewed attention to the writings of Alexis de Tocqueville, who is seen (not without reason) as the locus classicus for this subject. After all, it was Tocqueville who declared that "in democratic countries knowledge of how to combine is the mother of all other forms of knowledge . . . If men are to remain civilized or to become civilized, the art of association must develop and improve among them at the same speed as equality of conditions spreads."[2]

No non-contemporary writer is more frequently cited by American academic and politicians. But Tocqueville is more often quoted than understood. In this brief essay, I will try to place Tocqueville's discussion of voluntary associations in *Democracy in America* in what I believe to be its proper context and examine its relevance for contemporary politics.

POLITICAL ASSOCIATIONS

Tocqueville begins his discussion of voluntary organizations in democracies with politics rather than civil society.[3] His discussion of political association is less well known than that of civil association but, as we shall see, not less important.

Tocqueville distinguishes three types, or phases, of free political association—the aggregations of shared belief arising from free public speech, especially through the organs of mass communication such as newspapers; freedom of assembly; and most significantly, formal conventions organized around political parties or burning national issues. Free political associations serve as counterweights both to directly coercive concentrations of political power and to the more subtle but not less significant threat to democratic liberty that he famously labels the "tyranny of the majority" over the minds of democratic citizens.

Perhaps most surprising to contemporary readers is Tocqueville's emphasis on the threat posed by freedom of political association, or by its abuse. At one point he declares that "unlimited freedom of association must not be entirely identified with freedom to write. The former is both less necessary and more dangerous than the latter. A nation may set limits there without ceasing to be its own master; indeed, in order to remain its own master, it is sometimes necessary to do so."[4]

Our surprise abates when we appreciate the context of Tocqueville's concern. Full freedom of political association is a threat under two conditions: first, when the majority is excluded from political participation, so that an insurgent party can claim to represent the people against state institutions; second, when the differences among political factions or parties are fundamental. In these circumstances, free political associations are may be viewed as, or become, a form of "war on the government." In the United States, however, the majority (of adult white males) is able to participate in politics, and "differences of view are only matters of nuance." In these very different circumstances, far from threatening democratic government, unlimited freedom of political association helps secure it.[5]

In effect, Tocqueville presents a sketch of the empirical conditions under which parties or factions can be expected to serve as sources of peaceful and legitimate democratic opposition rather than revolutionary threats to the regime. It is worthy of note that in the one clear instance in U. S. history when political parties came to represent fundamental differences of political principle, the result was insurrection and civil war.

CIVIL ASSOCIATIONS

I turn now to Tocqueville's renowned discussion of civil associations. The context is set by his suggestion that while democratic peoples prize both liberty and equality, their desire for equality is more powerful: "They want equality in freedom, and if they cannot have that, they still want equality in slavery."[6] Unchecked and unmodified, the passion for equality constitutes a threat to liberty.

This threat manifests itself in two ways. First, to thwart noxious inequalities, societies may accept oppressive governments: a popular policy of anti-aristocratic leveling may trump economic and political liberties and even freedom of the mind.

The second temptation is more subtle. Social equality erodes bonds that depend on stability and hierarchy. The result is individualism, "a calm and considered feeling which disposes each citizen to isolate himself from the mass of his fellows and withdraw into the circle of family and friends." The resulting danger is both personal and social. On the personal level, every individual runs the risk of isolation and loneliness, the loss of essential human connection, "shut up in the solitude of his own heart." Socially, these egalitarian individuals tend to forget their debt to their ancestors and their responsibility to their descendents and to fall prey to the disabling illusion that "their whole destiny is in their own hands."[7]

If the passion for equality is the destiny of human beings in modernity, how can its dangerous excesses be checked? Tocqueville's suggestion is that free local institutions, responsible for the affairs of daily life, call into being the kinds of voluntary associations that can counteract the isolating effects of individualism. In the United States, the Founders used federalism to create regular occasions for local citizens to act in concert so that "every day they should feel that they depended on one another." As a general matter, local liberties "bring men constantly into contact, despite the instincts which separate them, and force them to help one another."[8]

Civil associations are as diverse as daily life itself. Americans form such associations for every conceivable practical purpose, religious and secular. Even more important are associations formed to "proclaim a truth or propagate some feeling by the encouragement of a great example."[9] Tocqueville offers a marvelous personal reflection that (against the odds) holds out the possibility of Franco-American cultural understanding:

> The first time that I heard in America that one hundred thousand men had publicly promised never to drink alcoholic liquor, I thought it more of a joke than a serious matter and for the moment did not see why these very abstemious citizens could not content themselves with drinking water by their own firesides. In the end I came to understand that these hundred thousand Americans, frightened by the progress of drunkenness around them, wanted to support sobriety by their patronage.[10]

There are important analogues to this kind of association in contemporary America; one thinks immediately of the Promise Keepers or even the Million Man March. But the temperance example illustrates the complexities of associational life. In spite of his considerable prescience, Tocqueville did not anticipate that the activity of bearing moral witness would be converted into a political program, a mass political movement, and ultimately legislative and constitutional change. Civil associations are not always parallel with, or replacements for, official politics; they can also serve as arenas for shaping public opinion and spurring concerted public action.

As we have seen, Tocqueville argues that the social consequences of egalitarianism make necessary the creation of voluntary associations. In aristocratic societies, the rich and powerful can spur action by mobilizing their retinues of dependents and hangers-on. In democratic societies, only voluntary associations can overcome the relative weakness of individual citizens, who can neither fend for themselves nor force others to act.[11]

In this context, one must ask whether the increasing concentration of wealth in market societies, at the onset of corporate industrial production a century ago and again today in the early phase of the information technology economy, alters the thrust of Tocqueville's analysis in ways that his acute observations of the Jacksonian economy did not allow him to anticipate. To the extent that large corporations and the super-rich have the quasi-aristocratic capacity to induce others to act, they occupy some of the social space that would otherwise be filled by voluntary activities. Much the same might be said of the large independent foundations into which the super-rich in the United States typically funnel a substantial portion of their wealth.

One must also ask whether this social space can be, or has been, usurped by the public sector. Tocqueville does anticipate and explore this issue. Faced with the weakness of individuals in egalitarian times, many of his contemporaries responded by advocating a larger and stronger government that "spread[s] its net ever wider." Tocqueville feared that this expansive administrative state could not carry out its self-appointed task and would eventuate in economic and social stultification. Even worse, it would produce a "vicious circle" that would undermine the independence, dignity, and liberty of citizens:

> The more government takes the place of associations, the more will individuals lose the idea of forming associations and need the government to come to their help. . . . The morals and intelligence of a democratic people would be in as much danger as its commerce and industry if ever a government wholly usurped the place of private associations.[12]

THE RELATIONSHIP BETWEEN POLITICAL AND CIVIL ASSOCIATIONS

Tocqueville's account of the relationship between political and civil associations is more subtle than that of many of his modern followers. His point of departure is the observation that in the United States of the 1830s, vigorous political and civil associations go together in a manner that is unlikely to be accidental. The question is the nature of the connection between them. Tocqueville's thesis is that each supports the other.

On the one hand, civil associations pave the way for political associations. The more individuals get used to the idea of coming together for economic, social, or moral purposes, the more they enhance their capacity to "pursue great aims in common."[13]

On the other hand, a free political system creates strong incentives for extensive political associations. People who might otherwise have led isolated lives have the desire to join forces and over time learn how to do so effectively, and "the advantages gained in important matters give them a practical lesson in the value of helping one another even in lesser affairs."[14] It is through political associations that Americans of every description "acquire a general taste for association and get familiar with the way to use [it]."[15] And thus, Tocqueville concludes, we may understand political associations as "great free schools in which all citizens come to be taught the general theory of association."[16]

Two important hypotheses flow from this argument, each with important implications for contemporary politics. In the first place, if Tocqueville's thesis is correct, it is a mistake to believe that civil society can remain strong as citizens withdraw from active engagement in political associations. Over time, the devitalization of the public sphere is likely to yield a privatized hyperindividualism that enervates the civil sphere as well.[17] While it is the case that excessive political centralization and administrative intrusion weakens civil society, the hydraulic vision of a civil society that expands as participatory democratic politics contracts is deeply misguided.

Second, autocrats of all stripes are mistaken if they believe that they can divert political interests into private civil endeavors. If free political expression is repressed, associational energies are likely to dwindle in the sphere of voluntary association as well, as individuals become isolated, privatized, and demoralized.[18]

This is not to suggest that political repression will necessarily fragment civil society. It matters how repression is carried out. If state institutions embark on a deliberate strategy of eliminating civil society by outlawing independent associations, bringing formally autonomous activities under state control, and sowing mistrust among citizens, then civil society will be gravely weakened. Russia is now grappling with the consequences of just such a strategy. But if quasi-independent civil associations are tolerated, the result may be a displacement of political energies into the civil sector. (Something of this sort took place in Poland.) For this reason, repressive regimes that do not totally squelch voluntary associations will frequently find it difficult to distinguish between genuinely civil activities and those that represent politics by other means—witness the treatment of the Falun Gong sect at the hands of the Chinese government.

CONCLUSION: THE USES OF CIVIL SOCIETY

This brief discussion should suffice to indicate the multiplicity of functions voluntary associations perform in contemporary regimes. These associations can serve as sites of resistance against tyranny and oppression. By strengthening social bonds, they can reduce the dangers of anomie. They can foster the bourgeois virtues that modern democratic societies need, and they can nourish the habits of civic engagement. Through internal dialogue and activities, they can help form opinions that shape deliberation in democratic public institutions. They provide vehicles for the non-instrumental expression of moral convictions as norms for the wider society. And of course, they offer opportunities for groups of citizens to conduct important public work through collective action outside the control of government.

In modern democratic societies, Tocqueville concludes, the principle of self-interest is bound to govern human action. The question is how self-interest is to be interpreted. Through their diverse functions and operations, civil associations help democratic citizens move from raw self-interest to "self-interest rightly understood," in part by teaching citizens that some sacrifice of self-interest is needed to preserve the rest. Self-interest rightly understood does not directly create virtue, but it does impose a discipline that shapes "orderly, moderate, careful, and self-controlled citizens."[19] It does not conduce to heroic virtue, but it does reduce the incidence of gross inhumanity. As checks on otherwise untrammeled individualism, civil associations serve the cause of liberty.

Or so Tocqueville argues. The question posed to contemporary democracies is whether these sources of moderation and decency still suffice. The relentless rise of individual choice as the central norm of modern societies has corroded both moral authority and the social structures that once reinforced it.[20] In the United States, where this tendency is farthest advanced, it is difficult to discern an effective counterweight to the powerful if peculiar understanding of liberty as untrammeled individual choice. The new century will test the proposition that this principle constitutes an adequate basis for a free society.

NOTES

1. For insight into the current debate, see Theda Skocpol and Morris P. Fiorina, eds., *Civic Engagement and American Democracy* (Washington, DC: Brookings, 1999); Robert K. Fullinwider, ed., *Civil Society, Democracy, and Civic Renewal* (Lanham, MD: Rowman & Littlefield, 1999); E. J. Dionne Jr., ed., *Community Works: The Revival of Civil Society in America* (Washington, DC: Brookings, 1998).

2. Alexis de Tocqueville, *Democracy in America*, George Lawrence, trans. (New York: Harper & Row, 1966), p. 517.

3. *Democracy in America*, volume 1, part II, chapter 4.

4. *Ibid*, p. 191.

5. *Ibid*, p. 194.

6. *Ibid*, p. 506.

7. *Ibid*, p. 506, 508.

8. *Ibid*, p. 511.

9. *Ibid*, p. 513.

10. *Ibid*, p. 516.

11. *Ibid*, p. 514.

12. *Ibid*, p. 515.

13. *Ibid*, p. 520.

14. *Ibid*, p. 521.

15. *Ibid*, p. 524.

16. *Ibid*, p. 522.

17. For a recent social scientific examination of this "top-down" relationship, see Wendy M. Rahn, John Brehm, and Neil Carlson, "National Elections as Institutions for Generating Social Capital," in Skocpol and Fiorina, eds, *Civic Engagement in American Democracy*.

18. *Democracy in America*, p. 523.

19. *Ibid*, p. 527.

20. On this point, see especially Alan Ehrenhalt, "Where Have All the Followers Gone?" in Dionne, ed., *Community Works*.

Part II

POLICY

Chapter Five

The Perils of Preemptive War (2002)

On June 1, 2002, at West Point, President Bush set forth a new doctrine for American security policy. The successful strategies of the Cold War era, he declared, are ill-suited to national defense in the 21st century. Deterrence means nothing against terrorist networks; containment will not thwart unbalanced dictators possessing weapons of mass destruction. We cannot afford to wait until we are attacked. In today's circumstances, Americans must be ready to take "pre-emptive action" to defend our lives and liberties.

Applied to Iraq, the case for preemption runs roughly as follows: we do not know whether Saddam Hussein has yet acquired nuclear weapons or transferred them to terrorists. It doesn't matter. We know that he's trying to get these weapons, and his past conduct suggests that he will use them against our interests. The probability of the worst case is low but hardly negligible. We cannot wait until one of his bombs, packed into a terrorist's suitcase, blows up Manhattan. We must act now—and do whatever it takes—to eliminate this threat.

After an ominous silence lasting much of the summer, a debate about U.S. policy toward Iraq has finally begun. Remarkably, Democrats are not party to it. Some agree with Bush administration hawks; others have been intimidated into acquiescence or silence. The Foreign Relations Committee hearings yielded questions rather than answers and failed to prod Democratic leaders into declaring their position. Meanwhile, Democratic political consultants are advising their clients to avoid foreign policy and to wage their campaigns on the more hospitable turf of corporate fraud and prescription drugs. The memory of the Gulf War a decade ago, when the vast majority of Democrats ended up on the wrong side of the debate, deters many from reentering the fray today.

The Democratic Party's abdication has left the field to Republican combatants—unilateralists versus multilateralists, ideologues versus "realists." The resulting debate has been intense but narrow, focused primarily on issues of prudence rather than principle.

This is not to suggest that the prudential issues are unimportant, or that the intra-Republican discord has been unilluminating. Glib analogies between Iraq and Afghanistan and cocky talk about a military "cakewalk" have given way to more sober assessments. President Bush's oft-repeated goal of "regime change" would likely require 150,000-200,000 U.S. troops, allies in the region willing to allow us to pre-position and supply them, and bloody street battles in downtown Baghdad. With little left to lose, Saddam Hussein might carry out a "Samson scenario" by equipping his Scuds with chemical or biological agents and firing them at Tel Aviv. Senior Israeli military and intelligence officials doubt that Prime Minister Ariel Sharon would defer to U.S. calls for restraint, as the Shamir government did during the Gulf War. Israeli retaliation could spark a wider regional conflagration.

Assume that we can surmount these difficulties. The Bush administration's goal of regime change is the equivalent of our World War II aim of unconditional surrender and would have similar post-war consequences. We would assume total responsibility for Iraq's territorial integrity, for the security and basic needs of its population, and for the reconstruction of its system of governance and political culture. This would require an occupation measured in years or even decades. Whatever our intentions, nations in the region (and elsewhere) would view our continuing presence through the historical prism of colonialism. The *Economist*, which favors a U.S. invasion of Iraq, nonetheless speaks of the "imperial flavour" of the occupation.

The risks would not end there. The administration and its supporters argue that the overthrow of Saddam Hussein would shift the political balance in our favor throughout the Middle East (including among the Palestinians). Henry Kissinger is not alone in arguing that the road to solving the Israeli-Palestinian conflict leads through Baghdad, not the other way around. More broadly, say the optimists, governments in the region would see that opposing the United States carries serious risk and that there is more to be gained from cooperating with us. Rather than rising up in injured pride, the Arab "street" would respect our resolve and move toward moderation, as would Arab leaders.

Perhaps so. But it does not take much imagination to conjure a darker picture, and the performance of our intelligence services in the region does not inspire confidence in the factual basis of the optimists' views. If a wave of public anger helped Islamic radicals unseat Pakistan's General Pervez Musharraf, for example, we would have exchanged a dangerous regime seeking nuclear weapons for an even more dangerous regime that possesses them.

All this and I have not yet mentioned potential economic and diplomatic consequences. Even a relatively short war would likely produce an oil price spike that could tip the fragile global economy into recession. Moreover, unlike the Gulf War, which the Japanese and Saudis largely financed, the United States would have to go it alone this time, with an estimated price tag of $60 billion for the war and $15-20 billion per year for the occupation.

Our closest allies have spoken out against an invasion of Iraq. Gerhard Schroeder, leading a usually complaisant Germany but locked in a tough re-election fight, has gone so far as to label this possibility an "adventure," sparking a protest from our ambassador. Some Bush administration officials seem not to believe that our allies' views matter all that much. Others argue, more temperately, that the Europeans and other protesters will swallow their reservations after the fact when they can see the military success of our action and its positive consequences. They may be right. But it is at least as likely that this disagreement will widen the already sizeable gap between European and American world-views. New generations of young people could grow up resenting and resisting America, as they did after Vietnam. Whether these trends in the long run undermine our alliances, they could have a range of negative short-term consequences, including diminished intelligence sharing and cooperation.

Republicans have at least raised these prudential issues. For the most part, however, they have ignored broader questions of principle. But these questions cannot be evaded. An invasion of Iraq would be one of the most fateful deployments of American power since World War II. A global strategy based on the new Bush doctrine of preemption means the end of the system of international institutions, laws, and norms that we have worked for more than half a century to build. To his credit, Kissinger recognizes this. He labels Bush's new approach "revolutionary" and declares that "regime change as a goal for military intervention challenges the international system." The question is whether this revolution in international doctrine is justified and wise.

I think not. What is at stake is nothing less than a fundamental shift in America's place in the world. Rather than continuing to serve as first among equals in the post-war international system, America would act as a law unto itself, creating new rules of international engagement without the consent of other nations. In my judgment, this new stance would ill serve the long-term interests of the United States.

There is a reason why President Bush could build on the world's sympathy in framing the U.S. response against Al Qaeda after September 11, and why his father was able to sustain such a broad coalition to reverse Saddam Hussein's invasion of Kuwait. In those cases our policy fit squarely within established doctrines of self-defense. By contrast, if we seek to overthrow Saddam

Hussein, we will act outside the framework of global security that we have helped create.

In the first place, we are a signatory to (indeed, the principal drafter of) the Charter of the United Nations. The Charter explicitly reserves to sovereign nations "the inherent right of individual or collective self-defense," but only in the event of armed attack. Unless the administration establishes Iraqi complicity in the terrorism of September 11, it cannot invoke self-defense, as defined by the Charter, as the justification for attacking Iraq. And if evidence of Iraqi involvement exists, the administration has a responsibility to present it to Congress, the American people, and the world, much as John F. Kennedy and Adlai Stevenson did to justify the U.S. naval blockade of Cuba during the missile crisis.

The broader structure of international law creates additional obstacles to an invasion of Iraq. To be sure, international law contains a doctrine of "anticipatory self-defense," and there is an ongoing argument concerning its scope. Daniel Webster, then Secretary of State, offered the single most influential statement of the doctrine in 1842: there must be shown "a necessity of self-defense . . . instant, overwhelming, leaving no choice of means, and no moment for deliberation." Some contemporary scholars adopt a more permissive view. But even if that debate were resolved in the manner most favorable to the Bush administration, the concept of anticipatory self-defense would still be too narrow to support an attack on Iraq: the threat to the United States from Iraq is neither sufficiently specific, nor clearly enough established, nor shown to be imminent.

The Bush doctrine of preemption goes well beyond the established bounds of anticipatory self-defense, as many supporters of the administration's Iraq policy privately concede. (They argue that the United States needs to make new law, using Iraq as a precedent.) If the administration wishes to argue that terrorism renders the imminence criterion obsolete, it must do what it has thus far failed to do—namely, show that Iraq has both the capability of harming us and a serious intent to do so. The abstract logical possibility that Saddam Hussein could transfer weapons of mass destruction to stateless terrorists is not enough. If we cannot make our case, the world will see "anticipatory self-defense" as an international hunting license.

Finally, we can examine the proposed invasion of Iraq through the prism of just war theories developed by philosophers and theologians over a period of centuries. One of its most distinguished contemporary exponents, Michael Walzer, puts it this way: first strikes can occasionally be justified before the moment of imminent attack, if we have reached the point of "sufficient threat." This concept has three dimensions: "a manifest intent to injure, a degree of active preparation that makes that intent a positive danger, and a general situation in which waiting, or doing anything other than fighting, greatly magnifies the risk." The potential injury, moreover, must be of the gravest possible nature: the loss of territorial integrity or political independence.

Saddam Hussein may well endanger the survival of his neighbors, but he poses no such risk to the United States. And he knows full well that complicity in a September 11–style terror attack on the United States would justify, and swiftly evoke, a regime-ending response. During the Gulf War, we invoked this threat to deter him from using weapons of mass destruction against our troops, and there is no reason to believe that this strategy would be less effective today. Dictators have much more to lose than do stateless terrorists; that's why deterrence directed against them has a good chance of working.

In its segue from Al Qaeda to Saddam Hussein, and from defense to preemption, the Bush administration has shifted its focus from stateless foes to state-based adversaries, and from terrorism in the precise sense to the possession of weapons of mass destruction. Each constitutes a threat. But they are not the same threat and do not warrant the same response. It serves no useful purpose to pretend that they are seamlessly connected, let alone one and the same.

The United Nations, international law, just war theory . . . it is not hard to imagine the impatience with which Bush administration policy-makers will greet arguments made on this basis. The first duty of every government, they will say, is to defend the lives and security of its citizens. The elimination of Saddam Hussein and, by extension, every regime that threatens to share weapons of mass destruction with anti-American terrorists, comports with this duty. To invoke international norms designed for a different world is to blind ourselves to the harsh necessities of international action in the new era of terrorism. Now that we have faced the facts about the axis of evil, it would be a dereliction of duty to shrink from their consequences for policy. Even if no other nation agrees, we have a duty to the American people to go it alone. The end justifies, indeed requires, the means.

These are powerful claims, not easily dismissed. But even if an invasion of Iraq succeeds in removing a threat here and now, it is not clear whether a policy of preemption would make us safer in the long run. Specifically, we must ask how the new norms of international action we employ would play out as nations around the world adopt them and shape them to their own purposes. (And they *will*; witness the instant appropriation of the United States' anti-terrorism rhetoric by Russia and India, among others.) It is an illusion to believe that the United States can employ new norms of action while denying the right of others to do so as well.

Also at stake are competing understandings of the international system and of our role within it. Some administration officials appear to believe that alliances and treaties are in the main counterproductive, constraining us from most effectively pursuing our national interest. Because the United States enjoys unprecedented military, economic, and technological preeminence, we can do best by going it alone. The response to these unilateralists is that there are many goals that we cannot hope to achieve without the cooperation of others. Pretending that we can exchanges short-term gains for long-term risks.

Even after we acknowledge the important distinctions between domestic and international politics, the fact remains: no push for international cooperation can succeed without international law and, therefore, without treaties that build the institutions for administering that law. This is one more reason, if one were needed, why the United States must resist the temptation to set itself apart from the system of international law. It will serve us poorly in the long run if we offer public justifications for an invasion of Iraq that we cannot square with established international legal norms.

We are the most powerful nation on earth, but we are not invulnerable. To safeguard our own security, we need the assistance of the allies whose doubts we scorn, and the protection of the international restraints against which we chafe. We must therefore resist the easy seduction of unilateral action. In the long run, our interests will be best served by an international system that is as law-like and collaborative as possible, given the reality that we live in a world of sovereign states.

Chapter Six

Some Arguments for
Universal Service (2004)

The purpose of this chapter is to offer civic arguments for a program of mandatory service. To the extent that circumstances permit, we should move toward a system of universal eighteen-month service for all high school graduates (and in the case of dropouts, all 18-year-olds) who are capable of performing it. Within the limits imposed by military manpower requirements, those subject to this system would be able to choose either military or full-time civilian service. (If all military slots were filled, then some form of civilian service would be the only option.) The cost of fully implementing this proposal (a minimum of $60 billion per year) would certainly slow the pace of implementation and might well impose a permanent ceiling on the extent of implementation. The best response to these constraints would be a lottery to which all are exposed and from which none except those unfit to serve can escape.

To understand the civic motivations for this proposal, I begin by reviewing some relevant history.

The Vietnam-era military draft was widely regarded as arbitrary and unfair, and it was held responsible for dissension within the military as well as the wider society. In the immediate wake of its disaster in Vietnam, the United States made an historic decision to end the draft and institute an All-Volunteer Force (AVF). On one level, it's hard to argue with success. The formula of high quality volunteers plus intensive training plus investment in state of the art equipment has produced by far the most formidable military in history. Evidence suggests that the military's performance, especially since 1990, has bolstered public trust and confidence. For example, a recent Gallup survey of public opinion trends since the end of the Vietnam War in 1975 indicates that while the percentage of Americans expressing confidence in religious leaders fell from 68 to 45 and from 40 to 29 for Congress, the percentage expressing confidence in the military rose from under 30 to 78. Among 18- to 29-year-olds, the confidence level rose from 20 to 64 percent. (Remarkably, these figures reflect sentiment in late 2002, *before* the impressive victory in Iraq.)

While these gains in institutional performance and public confidence are impressive, they hardly end the discussion. As every reader of Machiavelli (or the Second Amendment) knows, the organization of the military is embedded is larger issues of citizenship and civic life. It is along these dimensions that the decision in favor of the AVF has entailed significant costs. First, the AVF reflects, and has contributed to the development of, what I call *optional citizenship*, the belief that being a citizen involves rights without responsibilities and that we need do for our country only what we choose to do. Numerous studies have documented the rise of individual choice as the dominant norm of contemporary American culture, and many young people today believe being a good person—decent, kind, caring, and tolerant—is all it takes to be a good citizen. This duty-free understanding of citizenship is comfortable and undemanding; it is also profoundly mistaken.

Second, the AVF contributes to what I call *spectatorial citizenship*—the premise that good citizens need not be active but can watch others doing the public's work on their behalf. This spectatorial outlook makes it possible to decouple the question of whether *we* as a nation should do X from the question of whether *I* would do or participate in X. In a discussion with his students during the Gulf War, Cheyney Ryan, professor of philosophy at the University of Oregon, was struck by "how many of them saw no connection between whether the country should go to war and whether they would . . . be willing to fight in it." A similar disconnect exists today. Far higher percentages of young adults are supportive of the war against Iraq than would be willing to serve in it themselves.

Finally, the AVF has contributed to a widening gap between the orientation and experience of military personnel and that of the citizenry as a whole. This is an empirically contested area, but some facts are not in dispute. First, since the inauguration of the AVF, the share of officers identifying themselves as Republican has nearly doubled, from 33 to 64 percent. (To be sure, officers were always technically volunteers, but the threat of the draft significantly affected the willingness of young men to volunteer for officer candidacy.) Second, and more significantly, the share of elected officials with military experience has declined sharply. From 1900 through 1975, the percentage of members of Congress who were veterans was always higher than in the comparable age cohort of the general population. Since the mid-1990s, the congressional percentage has been lower, and it continues to fall.

Lack of military experience does not necessarily imply hostility to the military. Rather, it means ignorance of the nature of military service, as well as diminished capacity and confidence to assess critically the claims that military leaders make. (It is no accident that of all the post-war presidents, Dwight Eisenhower was clearly the most capable of saying no to the military's strategic assessments and requests for additional resources.)

For these reasons, among others, I believe that as part of a reconsideration of the relation between mandatory service and citizenship, we should review and revise the decision we made 30 years ago to institute an all-volunteer armed force. I hasten to add that I do not favor reinstituting anything like the Vietnam-era draft. It is hard to see how a reasonable person could prefer that fatally flawed system to today's arrangements. The question, rather, is whether feasible reforms could preserve the gains of the past thirty years while more effectively promoting active, responsible citizenship across the full range of our social, economic, and cultural differences.

My suggestion faces a threshold objection, however, to the effect that any significant shift back toward a mandatory system of military manpower would represent an abuse of state power. In a recent article, Judge Richard Posner drafts John Stuart Mill as an ally in the cause of classical liberalism — a theory of limited government that provides an "unobtrusive framework for private activities." Limited government so conceived, Posner asserts, "has no ideology, no 'projects,' but is really just an association for mutual protection." Posner celebrates the recent emergence of what he calls the "Millian center" — a form of politics that (unlike the left) embraces economic liberty and (unlike the right) endorses personal liberty, and he deplores modern communitarianism's critique of untrammeled personal liberty in the name of the common good. High on Posner's bill of particulars is the recommendation of some (not all) communitarians to reinstitute a draft.

Before engaging Posner's own argument, I should note that his attempt to appropriate Mill's *On Liberty* to support an anti-conscription stance is deeply misguided. To clinch this point, I need only cite a few of the opening sentences from Chapter Four, entitled "Of the Limits to the Authority of Society Over the Individual":

> [E]veryone who receives the protection of society owes a return for the benefit, and the fact of living in society renders it indispensable that each should be bound to observe a certain line of conduct toward the rest. This conduct consists, first, in not injuring the interests of one another, or rather certain interests which, either by express legal provision or by tacit understanding, ought to be considered as rights; *and secondly, in each person's bearing his share (to be fixed on some equitable principle) of the labors and sacrifices incurred for defending the society or its members from injury and molestation. These conditions society is justified in enforcing at all costs to those who endeavor to withhold fulfillment.*

Posner's view of Mill would make sense only if Mill had never written the words I have italicized.

It is not difficult to recast Mill's position in the vocabulary of contemporary liberal political thought. Begin with a conception of society as a system of cooperation for mutual advantage. Society is legitimate when the criterion of mutual advantage is broadly satisfied (versus, say, a situation in which the government or some group systematically coerces some for the sake of others). When society meets the standard of broad legitimacy, each citizen has a duty to do his/her fair share to sustain the social arrangements from which all benefit, and society is justified in using its coercive power when necessary to ensure the performance of this duty. That legitimate societal coercion may include mandatory military service in the nation's defense as well as other required activities that promote broad civic goals.

A counterargument urged by the late Robert Nozick that that we typically don't consent to the social benefits we receive and that the involuntary receipt of benefits does not trigger a duty to contribute. Mill anticipated, and rejected, that thesis, insisting that the duty to contribute does not rest on a social contract or voluntarist account of social membership. Besides, the argument Socrates imputes to the Laws in the *Crito* isn't unreasonable: if your society isn't a prison, if as an adult you remain when you have the choice to leave, then you have in fact accepted the benefits, along with whatever burdens the principle of social reciprocity may impose.

Robert Litan has recently suggested that citizens should be "required to give something to their country in exchange for the full range of rights to which citizenship entitles them." Responding in a quasi-libertarian vein, Bruce Chapman charges that this proposal has "no moral justification." Linking rights to concrete responsibilities is "contrary to the purposes for which [the United States] was founded and has endured." This simply isn't true. For example, the right to receive GI Bill benefits is linked to the fulfillment of military duties. Even the right to vote (and what could be more central to citizenship than that?) rests on law-abidingness; many states disenfranchise convicted felons during their period of incarceration and probation. As Litan points out, this linkage is hardly tyrannical moralism. Rather, it reflects the bedrock reality that "the rights we enjoy are not free" and that it takes real work—contributions from citizens—to sustain constitutional institutions.

Judge Posner contends that "conscription could be described as a form of slavery, in the sense that a conscript is a person deprived of the ownership of his own labor." If slavery is immoral, so is the draft. In a similar vein, Nozick once contended that "taxation of earnings from labor is on a par with forced labor." (If Nozick were right, then the AVF that Posner supports, funded as it is with tax dollars, could also be described as on a par with forced labor.)

Both Posner's and Nozick's arguments prove too much. If each individual's ownership of his or her own labor is seen as absolute, then society as such becomes impossible, because no political community can operate without resources, which must ultimately come from *someone*. Public choice theory predicts, and all of human history proves, that no polity of any size can subsist through voluntary contributions alone; the inevitable free riders must be compelled by law, backed by force, to do their part

Still, the proponents of a free market/individual choice model might reasonably argue that if a non-coercive approach to military and civilian service can get the job done, there are no valid grounds for legal compulsion. To understand the shortcomings of this argument, consider the analogy (or disanalogy) between national service and domestic law enforcement. The latter is divided into two subcategories: voluntary activities (there's no draft for police officers) and mandatory responsibilities (e.g., jury duty). Our current system of national service is all "police" and no "jury." If we conducted domestic law enforcement on that model of service, we'd have what might be called "The All-Volunteer Jury," in which we'd pay enough to ensure a steady flow of the jurors the law enforcement system requires to function.

There are two compelling reasons not to move in this direction. First, citizens who self-select for jury duty are unlikely to be representative of the population as a whole. Individuals who incur high opportunity costs (those who are gainfully employed, for example) would tend not to show up. The same considerations that militate against forced exclusion of racial and ethnic groups from jury pools should weigh equally against voluntary self-exclusion based upon income or employment status. (We should ask ourselves why these considerations do not apply to the composition of the military.)

Second, it is important for all citizens to understand that citizenship is an *office*, not just a *status*. As an office, citizenship comprises matters of both rights and duties — indeed, some matters that are both. Service on juries is simultaneously a right, in the sense that that there is a strong presumption against exclusion, and a duty, in the sense that there is a strong presumption against evasion. To move jury duty into the category of voluntary, compensated acts would be to remove one of the last reminders that citizenship is more than a legal status.

I would also offer an argument based on civic self-respect. From the standpoint of military competence, we might do just as well to engage foreigners (the All-Mercenary Armed Forces), as kings and princes did regularly during the 18th century. The cost might well be lower, and the military performance just as high. Besides, if we hire foreigners to pick our crops, why shouldn't we hire them to do our fighting?

Leaning against these arguments based on competence and convenience is a moral intuition: even if a mercenary army were reliable and effective, it would be wrong, perhaps shameful, to use our wealth to get non-citizens to do our fighting for us. This is something we ought to do for ourselves, as a self-respecting people. I want to suggest that a similar moral principle applies as well in the purely domestic sphere, among citizens.

Consider military recruitment during the Civil War. In April 1861 President Lincoln called for, and quickly received, 75,000 volunteers. But the expectation of a quick and easy Union victory was soon dashed, and the first conscription act was passed in March 1863. The act contained two opt-out provisions: an individual facing conscription could pay a fee of $300 to avoid a specific draft notice; and an individual could avoid service for the entire war by paying a substitute to volunteer for three years.

This law created a complex pattern of individual incentives and unanticipated social outcomes, such as anti-conscription riots among urban workers. Setting these aside, was there anything wrong in principle with these opt-out provisions? I think so. In the first place, there was an obvious distributional unfairness: the well-off could afford to avoid military service, while the poor and working class couldn't. Historian James McPherson observes that the slogan "a rich man's fight, but a poor man's war" had a powerful impact, particularly among impoverished Irish laborers already chafing against the contempt with which they were regarded by the Protestant elite. Second, even if income and wealth had been more nearly equal, there would have been something wrong in principle with the idea that dollars could purchase exemption from an important civic duty. As McPherson notes, this provision enjoyed a poor reputation after the Civil War, and the designers of the World War I–era Selective Service Act were careful not to repeat it.

We can now ask: what is the difference between the use of personal resources to opt *out* of military service and the impact of personal resources on the decision to opt *in*? My answer: as both a practical and a moral matter, less than the defenders of the current system would like to believe. To begin with, the decision to implement an AVF has had a profound effect on the educational and class composition of the U.S. military. During World War II and the Korean War—indeed, through the early 1960s—roughly equal percentages of high school and college graduates saw military service, and about one third of college graduates were in the enlisted (that is, non-officer) ranks. Today, enlisted men and women are rarely college graduates, and elite colleges other than the service academies are far less likely to produce military personnel of any rank, officer or enlisted. As a lengthy *New York Times* feature story recently put it, today's military "mirrors a working-class America." Most of the young men and women who are dying in Iraq represent working class families from small-town and rural America.

Many have argued that this income skew is a virtue, not a vice, because the military extends good career opportunities to young men and women whose prospects are otherwise limited. There's something to this argument, of course. But the current system purchases social mobility at the expense of social integration. Today's privileged young people tend to grow up hermetically sealed from the rest of society. Episodic volunteering in soup kitchens doesn't really break the seal. Military service is one of the few experiences that can.

The separation is more than economic. The sons and daughters of the upper middle classes grow up in a cultural milieu in which certain assumptions tend to be taken for granted. Often, college experiences reinforce these assumptions rather than challenging them. Since Vietnam, moreover, many elite colleges and universities have held the military at arms' length, ending ROTC curricula and banning campus-based military recruitment. As a Vietnam-era draftee, I can attest to the role military service plays in expanding mutual awareness across cultural lines. This process is not always pleasant or pretty, but it does pull against the smug incomprehension of the privileged.

In an evocative letter to his sons, Brookings scholar Stephen Hess reflects on his experiences as a draftee and defends military service as a vital socializing experience for children from fortunate families. His argument is instructive: "Being forced to be the lowest rank . . ., serving for long enough that you can't clearly see 'the light at the end of the tunnel,' is as close as you will ever come to being a member of society's underclass. To put it bluntly, you will feel in your gut what it means to be at the bottom of the heap. . . . Why should you want to be deprived of your individuality? You shouldn't, of course. But many people are, and you should want to know how this feels, especially if you someday have some responsibility over the lives of other people." It's a matter, not just of compassion, but of respect: "The middle class draftee learns to appreciate a lot of talents (and the people who have them) that are not part of the lives you have known, and, after military duty, will know again for the rest of your lives. This will come from being thrown together with—and having to depend on—people who are very different from you and your friends."

A modern democracy, in short, combines a high level of legal equality with an equally high level of economic and social stratification. It is far from inevitable, or even natural, that democratic leaders who are drawn disproportionately from the upper ranks of society will adequately understand the experiences or respect the contributions of those from the lower. Integrative experiences are needed to bring this about. In a society in which economic class largely determines residence and education and in which the fortunate will not willingly associate with the rest, only non-voluntary institutions cutting across class lines can hope to provide such experiences. If some kind of sustained mandatory service doesn't fill this bill, it is hard to see what will.

It is one thing to invoke civic arguments in favor of universal service, quite another to make them a practical reality. As we reconsider the all-volunteer model of recruitment for armed service, we should also return to President Clinton's vision of national service as a package of responsibilities and privileges available to every young American. The program known as Ameri-Corps has survived repeated efforts to strangle it in its cradle and now enjoys broad bipartisan support. It is time to put our civic money where our civic mouth is: to move steadily from today's quota of 70,000 full-time participants each year to a system in which there's a place for every young American who wants to serve his or her country. As the baby-boom generation ages into retirement, it wouldn't be a bad idea to expand current senior-oriented service programs as well, to give retirees a fuller opportunity to put their experience and skills to work for their country.

We have spent decades creating programs that enhance individual self-improvement, consumption, and choice. If we work as hard to foster an ethic of reciprocity, we can create a genuinely civic culture that summons forth, in the words of Abraham Lincoln, the better angels of our nature.

Chapter Seven

Ethics and Public Policy in a Pluralist Democracy: The Case of Human Embryo Research (2001)

A BRIEF POLITICAL HISTORY

For more than a quarter of a century, the issue of research on human embryos has been entangled in broader controversies over fetal research and abortion. During the late 1960s and early 1970s, policy makers at the National Institutes of Health convened a study panel to consider regulations covering fetal research. Publication of draft fetal research guidelines aroused little interest until the *Roe v. Wade* decision in 1973.

Soon afterwards, the issue moved from the bureaucratic arena (what one scholar calls the "science subgovernment") to the public domain, where it became a "small skirmish in the larger battle over abortion."[1] The *Washington Post* published a front-page article entitled "Live-Fetus Research Debated," which sparked national news coverage and a demonstration at NIH headquarters. In 1974, Congress suspended all federal support for non-therapeutic fetal research until a national commission developed appropriate ethical guidelines. Within a year, the commission had made its recommendations, and Secretary of Health and Human Services Caspar Weinberger was able to sign a set of regulations creating a federal ethics advisory board (EAB) whose review and advice would be needed to fund most categories of fetal research.

Among other matters, the EAB had jurisdiction over in vitro fertilization (IVF), which it considered between 1978 and 1980. In one report issued during that period, the EAB concluded that federal funding of IVF research, subject to certain safeguards, was ethically appropriate. The HHS Secretary took no action on that report, and the charter of the EAB lapsed in 1980, shortly before the election of Ronald Reagan. Repeated efforts between 1981 and 1993 to reconstitute the EAB all failed, and in the ensuing absence of EAB review, a "de facto moratorium" on federal funding of fetal research prevailed.

75

The election of Bill Clinton created a new situation. Within days of assuming the presidency in January 1993 he issued an executive order lifting the ban on fetal tissue research. In June, he signed into law the NIH Revitalization Act of 1993, which nullified the regulation requiring EAB review of embryo research proposals. The NIH had already received a number of proposals for research on "pre-implantation embryos" (embryos in early stages of development prior to implantation in the uterus) and soon received more. Rather than rushing to fund these proposals, however, the NIH Director, Harold Varmus, established an external panel to review the ethical issues raised by the use of human pre-implantation embryos in research and the recommended guidelines for the funding and conduct of such research.

The Human Embryo Research Panel, whose nineteen members included philosophers, theologians, and legal scholars as well as research scientists, met five times between February and August of 1994. Early on, there were indications that its proceedings would be carefully monitored and that its recommendations would prove politically controversial. On June 16, 1994, Varmus received a letter signed by thirty-five members of Congress posing a series of legal and ethical questions concerning the panel's work. The tone and content of these questions made it clear that the letter was intended as a warning-shot.[2] Just five days later, Varmus responded with a lengthy description of the panel's purposes and procedures. He defended the panel as an appropriate means to carry out the intent of Congress in the NIH Revitalization Act of 1993 and assured the legislators that the panel was carefully considering the kinds of ethical issues that troubled them.[3] Later, the members of Congress responded to Varmus with another letter stating that in their view, his letter raised more questions than it answered. They were particularly troubled by the panel's apparent failure to include embryos within the purview of human subjects entitled to a wide range of protections during the conduct of research.[4]

The Human Embryo Research Panel released its report on September 27, 1994, sparking the events that constitute the primary focus of this essay.

THE REPORT AND ITS AFTERMATH

The Panel's thoughtful and detailed report dealt with issues ranging from scientific, medical, and ethical issues in pre-implantation embryos research to guidelines for such research and specific categories of activities that should qualify for (or be denied) federal funding. The Report's recommendations were based on three principal considerations:

- The promise of human benefit from research is significant, carrying great potential benefit to infertile couples, to families with genetic conditions, and to individuals and families in need of effective therapies for a variety of diseases.

- Although the pre-implantation human embryos warrants serious moral consideration as a developing form of human life, it does not have the same moral status as infants and children. This is because of the absence of developmental individuation in the pre-implantation embryos, the lack of even the possibility of sentience and most other qualities considered relevant to the moral status of persons, and the very high rate of natural mortality at this stage.

- In the continued absence of Federal funding and regulation in this area, pre-implantation human embryos research, which has been and is being conducted without Federal funding and regulation, would continue without consistent ethical and scientific review. It is in the public interest that the availability of Federal funding and regulation should provide consistent ethical and scientific review for this area of research.[5]

The question of ethically acceptable sources of pre-implantation embryos was, as the Report makes clear, one of the most difficult issues the Panel had to consider. There was a broad consensus among Panel members that embryos remaining from IVF treatments and donated by women or couples (the so-called "spares") could be used for research. But the Panel wrestled with the issue of whether it was ethically permissible to create embryos expressly for research purposes, without the intent or expectation that they would ever be implanted and develop into infants. The Panel believed that it should approach this issue by balancing the health and safety of men, women, and children against the moral respect due the pre-implantation embryo. It concluded that while the needs of men, women, and children should be given priority, the moral status of the pre-implantation embryos should limit their use to the most compelling circumstances: when the research cannot otherwise be conducted, or when it is necessary for the validity or statistical power of a study that is potentially of outstanding scientific and therapeutic value. In no case should research be conducted on embryos beyond the fourteenth day of development, at which point irreversible individuation typically occurs.[6]

This recommendation did not enjoy unanimous support. Patricia King, a professor of law and one of the Panel's co-chairs, dissented in part:

> The prospect that humanity might assume control of life creation is unsettling and provokes great anxiety. The fertilization of human oocytes for research purposes is unnerving because human life is being created solely for human use. I

do not believe that this society has developed the conceptual frameworks necessary to guide us down this slope. . . . At the very least, we should proceed with extreme caution. Perhaps the public's concerns can be allayed over time with the development of appropriate conceptual frameworks. In any event, the public must be convinced that such actions are necessary to obtain significant benefits for humankind and that the research will be responsibly conducted.[7]

King was among the first to raise an issue that became central in the next few months—the role of public opinion in a democracy. In a benevolent dictatorship, the claim that a proposed course of action will promote the public interest would (if true) suffice to legitimate that course of action. But in a democracy, there is no class of Platonic guardians. The people must decide for themselves whether to accept or reject proposed public acts. Scientific and medical experts may seek to shape and inform public judgment, but they cannot substitute themselves for it. The fact that the public finds a proposed course of action ethically "unsettling" or "unnerving" is a matter of legitimate consequence in a democracy—even if the public cannot articulate doubts with the kind of conceptual clarity demanded by moral philosophers.

Within a few days it became clear that King was not alone in her doubts and that a firestorm was developing. The disapproval of anti-abortion activists was to be expected. What was not expected was the forceful intervention of the mainstream media, spearheaded by the *Washington Post*. In a lead editorial, the *Post* blasted the Panel's recommendation:

The creation of human embryos specifically for research that will destroy them is unconscionable. The government has no business funding it. . . . Is there a line that should not be crossed even for scientific or other gain, and if so where is it? . . . In approving the funding of the purposeful creation of human embryos for any experiments the panel took a step too far.[8]

The Post's editorial was swiftly followed by a torrent of editorial, op-ed pieces, and letters to the editor in newspapers around the country. Meanwhile, alarm-bells were going off in the White House, where I was then serving as Deputy Assistant to President Clinton for Domestic Policy. The issue had clearly moved out of the inner workings of the bureaucracy into the public arena. The President would be held accountable for the actions of the executive branch.

To ensure that the issue would be carefully monitored and that the President would receive informed advice, an ad hoc working group was established, led by the chief of staff (Leon Panetta), the deputy chief of staff (Harold Ickes), and the senior advisor for policy (George Stephanopoulos). The working group included representatives of the Vice President's office, the

First Lady's office, the Counsel's office, the Office of Science and Technology Policy (OSTP), and the Domestic Policy Council (DPC), among others. (I served as the lead DPC representative.)

The day after the publication of the Panel's report, John Gibbons, the Assistant to the President for Science and Technology, wrote a memo to Panetta summarizing the procedures NIH would employ to review the report before reaching final recommendations. (Throughout the fall, the OSTP vigorously represented the views of the scientific community.) In response to a request from the Deputy Chief of Staff, and drawing on my academic background in moral and political philosophy, I summarized the ethical issues raised by the report. Joel Klein, the Deputy Counsel, took the lead on legal issues. On November 9, 1994, Harold Varmus, the NIH Director, came to the White House to give the working group a detailed briefing on the scientific issues. On November 21, Klein and Gibbons wrote a memo to Panetta analyzing the advantages and disadvantages of three options: full support for the Panel's recommendation, rejection of its recommendation concerning embryos created expressly for research purposes, and an outright ban on all federal funding for human embryo research. The full working group met several times, and members conferred informally on a regular basis.

By late November, we had reached two conclusions: first, that it would be very difficult to offer a compelling public justification for the Panel's recommendation that the federal government should fund the creation of embryos specifically for research purposes; and second, that the matter had to be resolved decisively. We were working against a deadline: the Advisory Council to the NIH Director was meeting in early December to consider the Panel's recommendations. We expected the Advisory Council to ratify those recommendations and advise the Director to accept them, which we assumed he would—perhaps the same day. So we recommended to the President that he personally intervene to prohibit the NIH from funding the creation of human embryos specifically for research purposes.

The President accepted our advice. In a written order released December 2, 1994 (the day of the Advisory Council's meeting), he acknowledged his appreciation for the work of the NIH committees and recognized the important scientific and medical benefits that could flow from research on human embryos. Nevertheless, citing "profound ethical and moral questions as well as issues concerning the appropriate allocation of federal funds," the President declared that "I do not believe that Federal funds should be used to support the creation of human embryos for research purposes, and I have directed that the NIH not allocate any resources for such research."[9]

In response to numerous press inquiries, members of the President's staff made it clear that this order referred only to embryos created solely and specifically for research purposes. The President had no intention of challenging the scientific consensus in favor of funding research on embryos created in the course of normal IVF procedures.

The President's distinction between the two categories of embryos was criticized from two very different directions. Many members of the scientific community (including the President's own science advisor) saw no distinction, particularly when vital experiments cannot proceed without research embryos. If research on spares is acceptable, why not research on embryos created for that purpose?

Leaders of the Catholic Church also denied the relevance of the distinction, but they drew the opposite policy conclusion. Cardinal Keeler, the President of the National Council of Catholic Bishops, wrote that

> a hard-and-fast distinction between 'spare' and 'research' embryos is untenable
> . . . this distinction means that human embryos cannot be created as part of a federally funded experiment, but can be manipulated and destroyed so long as they come from outside the federal project. Such a policy—that government may not use tax dollars to create life but only to destroy it—defies all moral logic.[10]

Despite these criticisms, I remain convinced that President Clinton's position is sound and prudent. In the following section of this article, I offer a sketch of the considerations that appeared compelling to most members of the White House working group and ultimately to the President.

PRACTICAL AND MORAL CONSIDERATIONS IN PUBLIC DECISION-MAKING

Deliberation never begins with a blank slate. Over the past two decades, all 50 states and many foreign countries have considered human embryo research and have passed legislation to regulate it. While every foreign country allows in vitro fertilization procedures, the vast majority impose significant restrictions on embryo research. (Of the eleven countries surveyed by the Panel, only four permitted research as extensive as the Panel proposed, and one banned it altogether.) These worldwide deliberations created a body of shared scientific, ethical, and institutional propositions from which U.S. policy makers at the federal level were able to draw.[11]

In addition to this legislative and policy background, members of the White House working group identified what the philosopher John Rawls has called "provisional fixed points"—specific practical judgments that fall short of certainty but enjoy widespread (not necessarily unanimous) support and are entrenched in our public culture. Four such judgments seemed especially pertinent.

First: we determined that a key "fixed point" was the distinction between abortion and contraception. While we recognized that from an ethical (as opposed to legal) standpoint the issue of abortion remains unsettled in American public culture, this is not the case for most forms of contraception, which enjoy broad public support. We were therefore unwilling to embrace any position the logic of which implied the ethical rejection of contraceptive strategies such as intra-uterine devices. (In this respect, we concurred with the Panel's reasoning.[12])

Second: we assumed that in vitro fertilization procedures (in roughly their current form) are ethically appropriate. The purpose of these procedures— enabling otherwise infertile women and couples to have healthy, normal children—is ethically valid, as is what is necessary to achieve this purpose, including the fertilization of more embryos than can be used for possible implantation.

Third: we distinguished between private conduct and public funding. Taking our cue from the long running controversy over federal support for abortions conducted under the aegis of Medicaid, we concluded that it was ethically coherent for the government to refrain from funding an activity that was legally permissible. It is one thing for the government to respect the liberty of individuals, but a very different matter for the government to act in ways that imply support for particular choices that individuals make in the exercise of their liberty. Government funding is not an ethically neutral act; it implies a degree of endorsement, and it implicates every taxpaying citizen in the funded activities. In circumstances of deep moral division, it is typically unwise for the government to move beyond legal acquiescence (which is itself controversial) to material support.

Finally: we assumed (as did the Panel) that it was appropriate to impose ethical limits on the conduct of scientific inquiry. We were well aware of the long historic link between the process of scientific discovery and the betterment of the human condition. We were also aware of the fact that at various points in that history, ethical and theological objections to particular scientific procedures (such as the dissection of cadavers) had been swept aside, to the long-term advantage of our species and with moral consequences retrospectively judged to be acceptable. Nonetheless, in the wake of events such as the Nazi experiments on human subjects and the Tuskegee experiment (for which President Clinton has apologized on behalf of the American people), most people believe that science cannot be treated as ethically autonomous. The premise "Experiment X is essential for the pursuit of knowledge" is not sufficient to warrant the conclusion that "Experiment X is ethically acceptable." That is the case even if the knowledge to be gained is potentially of great benefit to humankind.

There are two different ways in which ethical considerations might limit scientific inquiry. One is a kind of balancing test in which ethical considerations are placed on the deliberative scales along with other considerations, such as the practical importance of the knowledge to be gained. This is the procedure the Panel employed in reaching its conclusion about the creation of human embryos for research purposes: the large potential benefits were held to outweigh the ethical costs of using embryos whose moral status is lower than that of actual human beings.

But there is another way in which ethical considerations can constrain scientific inquiry. These considerations can serve as side-constraints—that is, as absolute barriers to a particular course of action, whatever the projected benefits of that course may be. (Immanuel Kant's injunction to act so as to treat humanity as an end in itself and never as means alone is one important basis for this way of thinking.) From this standpoint, the use of a balancing test is ethically inappropriate, because it falsely assumes that the ethical considerations in question can be "traded off" against others. Notably, the Panel was willing to employ a version of the side-constraint strategy, rooted in widely held moral beliefs, to address issues such as cloning: "The notion of cloning an existing human being, or of making 'carbon copies' of an existing embryo, appears repugnant to members of the public. Many members of the Panel share this view, and see no justification for Federal funding of research . . . for this purpose."[13]

The question of which ethical strategy is to be preferred cannot be detached from the features of specific controversies. When the issue involves experimentation on human subjects without their consent, most people consider the balancing test to be wildly inappropriate. (Could any projection of scientific value have justified the Tuskegee experiments?) Matters are more difficult when (as in the dispute over embryo research) there is sharp disagreement over the moral status of the experimental subject. Nonetheless, in considering the issue of embryo creation for research, many members of the White House working group came to believe that the side-constraint strategy of ethical reasoning was more appropriate than the balancing test the Panel had used, and that public objections to embryo creation for research purposes were as intense and as plausible as were their objections to cloning.

In reaching this conclusion, we were aware of the pitfalls of relying on moral sentiments and intuitions (which some of us came to call the "yuck factor"). In the past, after all, large numbers of people have expressed their repugnance for scientific procedures and social practices that are now widely accepted. In some cases, "natural" sentiments were invoked to defend practices (such as prohibitions on interracial marriage) that could not be rationally defended.

Still, officials in a democracy who act in the name of the people must begin by taking public sentiments seriously. Of course, our responsibility did not end there. If we had concluded that the people were clearly mistaken, we would have had the obligation to enter into a public dialogue with them in an effort to change their minds. But while we recognized a range of plausible views on the status of human embryos, it was not clear to us that the center of gravity of public opinion was in error. It was therefore entitled to a substantial measure of democratic respect.

Many of us were fortified in our view by a consideration that Patricia King had raised in her dissent. Our society, she suggested, has not yet developed the conceptual apparatus needed to deal with embryo research in a nuanced way. If so, then the absence of a hard-and-fast side-constraint is likely to produce a slippery slope in which more and more research is considered legitimate, at least within the scientific community. To be sure, the Panel itself sought to construct one clear barrier—the fourteen day limit. But along with a number of editorial writers, we were not reassured by indications that the Panel was not fully committed to that limit. The crucial passage of its Report reads, "For the present, research involving human embryos should not be permitted beyond the time of the usual appearance of the primitive streak *in vivo* (14 days)."[14] This seemed to us symptomatic of the fact that most members of the scientific community were chafing against limits to research and that it was therefore necessary to clarify and strengthen those limits.

The White House working group disagreed with the Panel on another key issue—the nature of the dialogue appropriate for public reflection in a liberal democracy. In an effort to define a key element of this dialogue, John Rawls suggests the employment of scientific reasoning "when not controversial." The Panel cited Rawls but dropped his qualification:

> Public policy employs reasoning that is understandable in terms that are independent of a particular religious, theological, or philosophical perspective, and it requires a weighing of arguments in the light of the best available information and scientific knowledge.[15]

One may well wonder whether there are any such terms. And even if there are, it is by no means clear that they define the limits of acceptable public discourse in a constitutional democracy. Along with many philosophers, President Clinton did not accept the Panel's definition. He believed (and continues to believe) in a more robust role for faith-based arguments in the public arena. From this perspective, the challenge of public dialogue is not to screen out religious and metaphysical commitments in the name of an elusive "neutral" policy Esperanto, but rather to find ways of dealing with the deep differences we inevitably (and properly) bring into the public arena.

This is in no way to denigrate the public importance of scientific arguments. Along with the Panel, the White House working group did its best to understand the scientific research process and key findings. We concluded that while science frequently delimits the range of acceptable policy choices, it rarely prescribes a specific alternative.

Consider, for example, scientific findings concerning the onset of genuine individuation in embryo development. For several days after fertilization, embryonic cells are undifferentiated and capable of developing in a range of directions. Moreover, these cells do not form part of an organized whole; one or more of them can be removed without affecting the later development of the fetus. Up to about fourteen days after fertilization, a single embryo can split into twins (or higher-order multiple births), a capacity that ends only with the appearance of the "primitive streak" that definitively establishes the embryo's head/tail and left/right orientation.[16]

So far, so good; but what policy conclusions follow from these facts? Consider what might seem a far-fetched analogy. Suppose you are told that either a single infant or identical twins have been locked in a closet. Would you be justified in conducting an experiment (say, on the composition of the air in the room) that could jeopardize the well-being of whoever is behind the closed door? What is the moral import of your ignorance of the exact number of individuals at risk? Or suppose you are assured that a particular experiment will have no adverse effect on the development of the infant(s). Does it follow that you are at liberty to conduct a different experiment that would have such an effect? At best, the issue of individuation is embedded in the broader question of the moral status of the developing embryo. But this question (unlike individuation) cannot be answered in purely scientific terms.

Lurking behind these conceptual questions was an eminently political issue: when judgments concerning scientific research are contested, who should decide? Many scientists believe that these conflicts should be resolved within the scientific community itself. This proposition is exposed to two objections. First, as we have seen, to the extent that the conflicts revolve around more than science, they cannot be fully resolved through scientific procedures and arguments. And second, to the extent that the issue is not the liberty of scientific inquiry but rather (as in embryo research) the disposition of public funds, the public has a legitimate interest in the decisions made by elected and appointed officials.

Once an issue is subject to political determination, new considerations come into play. For example, it becomes important to ask whether a position can be effectively explained to the public. In a democracy, if you can't frame solid public arguments for your position, you have good reason not to proceed. As the chairman of the Panel, Steven Muller, himself acknowledged, "by a huge majority, the public has no idea what *ex utero* or pre-implantation human embryo research means or what it involves. But it does, to most people, sound terrible."[17] For this reason, among others, the White House working group feared a political backlash: if we accepted the Panel's full recommendation, adverse congressional and public reaction might well lead to the continued cutoff of all funding for embryo research. We didn't want this to happen, and we didn't see how the aims of the scientific community would be served by this outcome.

The White House working group was acting in a context of deep moral divisions, within which a neutral language was unavailable and full consensus unachievable. There was, we thought, a moral imperative to seek a defensible compromise based on the ethical center of gravity of the arguments, the long-term best interests of the country, and the common sense of the people.

THE OUTCOME: THE CENTER DID NOT HOLD

In the end, the White House working group's effort to locate a viable middle ground did not succeed. As part of a temporary spending measure, the president was compelled to accept a rider banning all federal funding for embryo research.

Why did our efforts fail? The proximate cause was surely the November 1994 congressional elections, which brought to power a Republican majority strongly backed by Christian conservatives. Not surprisingly, this new majority was not disposed toward compromise and viewed the embryo research issue through the prism of a highly polarized abortion debate.

The Clinton administration also contributed to this result, however. The administration came to power in 1993 determined to reverse the restrictive abortion policies of the previous twelve years, a goal fervently advocated by core Democratic constituencies. Especially during 1993 and 1994, the administration was not in a mood to go slow on this issue. Its first acts in January of 1993 included pro-choice executive orders, and it pushed the NIH Revitalization Act of 1993 in part to nullify research restraints seen as stemming from pro-life pressures. So conservatives had some reason to doubt that the administration was really interested in serving as an honest broker or in seeking honorable compromise on embryo research issues.

Ultimately, I believe, the failure of the center to hold was rooted in a basic structural feature of contemporary American politics. When an issue becomes sufficiently visible to engage the attention of a mass public, the moderation and common sense of the people as a whole will typically favor middle-ground approaches. On the other hand, when an issue is contested principally among political elites and organized interest groups, positions at the far ends of the spectrum tend to predominate. (This is the case because during the past generation, the political parties have become more polarized and single-issue groups with intense points of view have proliferated.)

Despite numerous news stories and editorials during September and October of 1994, human embryo research did not engage the attention of the electorate as a whole and did not function as a voting issue in November of that year. Not surprisingly, the issue subsequently became the subject of a tug-of-war between the executive branch and the congressional majority, with most of the American people firmly on the sideline. This was a formula for winner-take-all politics rather than compromise, and so it proved.

CONCLUSION: THE MORAL STATUS OF THE PRE-IMPLANTATION EMBRYO

So much for the politics of the core issue raised by the President's order—the distinction between "spare" and "research" embryos. But what about its merits?

In a thoughtful review of the issues published in the Catholic journal *Commonweal*, Susan Ellis and Gordon Marino commented as follows:

> It is hard to imagine that the clock will be turned back on IVF. Consequently, a large number of embryos, which can either be discarded or used for research purposes, and then discarded, will continue to be produced. It is often argued with some cogency that in light of the substantial benefits that could come from doing research on these never-to-be-implanted embryos, it is nothing less than a sin not to use them for research purposes. If, however, we are willing to do research on embryos solely because they are no longer intended for implantation, then we are in effect stating that the moral status of the embryo does not depend upon its intrinsic properties, but rather upon the intention that others have for it. . . . If it is morally meet to experiment upon embryos no longer intended for implantation, then there must not be any morally compelling reason to protect embryos, period. . . . If one cluster of embryos is not entitled to the rights and protections of personhood, why should another be?[18]

These are powerful arguments, but they prove too much. In recent polls, roughly 80 percent of Americans approve of abortion in cases of rape, versus only 20 percent who approve of it for sex selection of children. Put more generally: about one-fifth of the population disapprove of abortion under virtually all circumstances; about one-fifth approve under virtually all circumstances; about three-fifths believe that the circumstances of conception and the intention of the agent make a crucial difference. It is not necessarily a sign of moral incoherence to believe that considerations other than the moral status of the fetus are pertinent to the moral quality of the act of abortion. Why isn't this the case, mutatis mutandis, for embryo research?

Ellis and Marino acknowledge what the White House working group noted—that the American people have passed an affirmative moral judgment on IVF procedures, the intention of which they applaud. But through a double effect, these procedures generate fertilized oocytes that are not immediately implanted in the primary recipient and are unlikely ever to be implanted subsequently. Ex hypothesi, the generation of these embryos—which might have been implanted but were not—is delimited by the intention of facilitating otherwise unattainable human procreation. Research on these embryos takes place under the moral aegis of this intention. By contrast, the creation of embryos for research purposes occurs under different moral auspices and summons up the centuries-old fear of the quest for scientific knowledge unchecked by natural or ethical limits.

It is true that (as Cardinal Keeler and others have charged) this conceptual distinction can be erased in practice: "For if in vitro fertilization clinics may not use federal funds to create 'research embryos' solely for the purpose of research, they can easily fertilize more embryos at the outset than are needed for 'reproductive' use by infertile couples—thus ensuring that they will have as many embryos as they want for research."[19] But this is precisely the kind of abuse that (as the Panel rightly suggested) could be addressed through the enhanced oversight that would accompany federal funding of embryo research.

It is revealing that in its final report, the Panel encounters considerable difficulty in justifying the creation of embryos solely for research purposes. After summarizing a range of moral objections to this practice, the Panel keeps its distance from positions that equate the moral status of research-only embryos with IVF embryos and instead offers a purely consequentialist defense: without research-only embryos, various forms of fertility research would be harder (perhaps impossible) to conduct.[20] This line of argument will persuade only those who already accept the idea that in the area of embryo research the end justifies the means. It does not directly engage, or counter, arguments based on moral side-constraints—for example, on the claim that the creation of embryos solely for research purposes is "inherently disrespectful of human life."[21]

In the end, I believe, we must grapple with a multiplicity of moral considerations, each of which is relevant to embryo research and none of which is dispositive. Claims resting on the moral status of the embryo, on the manner of its coming into being, and on the consequences of conducting (or not conducting) research all have weight. Carried to extremes, moral positions that urge us to ignore consequences ("let justice reign, though the earth perishes"[22]) lack credibility. On the other hand, there is a powerful presumption in favor of treating embryos carefully and with respect, as what the Panel itself calls a "developing form of human life." In my judgment, the Panel fails to make a compelling case that the consequences of not creating embryos for research purposes would be so negative as to rebut or override this presumption. But because this judgment rests on moral deliberation—a balancing of incommensurable moral considerations—rather than a logically compelling argument, others may disagree. In this respect (among others), the gap between moral and political decision-making may be narrower than many suppose.

NOTES

1. Steven Maynard-Moody, "Managing Controversies over Science: The Case of Fetal Research," *Journal of Public Administration Research and Theory* 5 (1995): 10.

2. Letter of Rep. Robert K. Dornan et al. to Dr. Harold Varmus, June 16, 1994.

3. Letter of Harold Varmus to Rep. Robert K. Dornan, June 21, 1994.

4. Letter of Rep. Robert K. Dornan et al. To Dr. Harold Varmus, September 1, 1994.

5. *Final Report of the Human Embryo Research Panel*, National Institutes of Health, September 27, 1994, p. 2.

6. *Report*, p. 4.

7. *Report*, p. 97.

8. *Washington Post*, October 2, 1994, C6.

9. Statement by the President, The White House, December 2 1994.

10. Letter of December 7, 1994, to President Clinton.

11. For the specifics, see Lori B. Andrews, "State Regulation of Human Embryo Research," and Andrews and Nanette Elster, "Cross-cultural Analysis of Policies Regarding Human Embryo Research" (papers commissioned by the Human Embryo Research Panel).

12. *Report*, p. 46.

13. *Report*, p. 94.

14. *Report*, p. 3; emphasis added.

15. *Report*, pp. 50-51.

16. See *Report*, pp. 20-22 and 107; also Peter Singer et al., ed., *Embryo Experimentation* (Cambridge: Cambridge University Press, 1990), chapters 1, 5, and 6.

17. Quoted in *Christianity Today*, January 9, 1995, p. 38.

18. *Commonweal*, December 2, 1994, p. 9

19. Letter to President Clinton, December 7, 1994.

20. *Report*, pp. 54-56.

21. *Report*, p. 53.

22. A rough translation of the Latin maxim, "Fiat justitia, pereat mundus," quoted frequently and approvingly by Immanuel Kant.

Chapter Eight

Some Proposals to Help Parents: A Progressive Perspective (2002)

The National Parenting Association has asked me help spur discussion on proposals to assist parents. But before I reach policy specifics, let me offer some personal reflections that may provide a framework for deliberations across ideological as well as partisan lines. Although I spend a great deal of time in dialogue with conservatives of good will (and there are many), I address these remarks especially to potential members of what might become a new progressive coalition.

One of my early ventures in national politics was an extended stint (June 1982–November 1984) as issues director in Walter Mondale's presidential campaign. That was a formative and deeply sobering experience. By the end, it was clear to me that the Democratic Party had—with the best of intentions—allowed itself to become a coalition of the top and the bottom (or as someone unkindly put it, "the overeducated and the undereducated"), with limited appeal to ordinary working families. I came to the conclusion that the party had lost touch with both the material interests and the moral sentiments of those families and that it would take a systematic, long-term effort to re-forge the connection. My guiding thesis was simple: we could not hope to regain majority support for a progressive program unless our economic and social policies rested (and were seen to rest) on moral premises that average families could accept.

While it was misleading, I believed, to divide the public agenda into "moral" and "economic" issues (for the simple reason that many economic questions have an overtly moral dimension), I argued that Democrats would have to restrain their tendency toward economic reductionism. That is, they would have to recognize that while some morally-laden disputes involve economic issues, others of equal human importance and political salience do not.

89

In that context, I came to advocate programs such as the Earned Income Tax Credit, which based income support on work. I also began speaking out on the importance of stable, intact families for children, neighborhoods, and our society and on the imperative for progressives to support programs to assist and strengthen such families.

At the beginning, my efforts were poorly received. I vividly remember a Democratic Party conclave in the fall of 1986 when my profamily remarks created such a firestorm among feminists and welfare-rights advocates that the meeting's leaders, including the chair of the DNC, felt compelled to publicly distance themselves from me. But the center of gravity of the discussion gradually shifted, as more Democrats and progressives got comfortable with the idea that support for stable, intact families did not mean either restoring patriarchy or anathematizing single mothers. Bill Clinton's embrace of a public vocabulary rooted in the moral mainstream accelerated this convergence. In a recent essay, Theda Skocpol writes:

> Some may feel that it is best to avoid talking about families, lest we exacerbate racially-charged divisions between dual- and single-parent families. But I disagree. Family-friendly conditions are vital for both sets of families. And progressives need not adopt a morally relativist stance. We can champion moral understandings and practical measures that acknowledge the complexities that all Americans live with on a daily basis. Most people accept that two married parents are best for children, even though each of us is personally acquainted with mothers or fathers who have to soldier on outside this ideal situation. As policies are formulated, progressives can acknowledge the tension between ideals and second-best necessities.[1]

Speaking as a charter "New Democrat," I would not change a single word of this statement, offered by one of our country's most distinguished social democratic scholar-activists. I hope (and believe) that it can become a point of consensus within an emerging twenty-first-century progressive coalition.

A second framing observation: during the past generation, social policy discussion has been dominated (and distorted) by the corrosive debate over welfare, while fiscal policy has been driven by the budget deficit. Whatever one thinks of the 1996 welfare bill and the 1997 balanced budget agreement, their passage meant that this long unfortunate cycle, which placed progressives on the defensive, has come to an end. As President Clinton anticipated, the new welfare regime shifted the responsibility (and burden of proof) to those who have insisted that adequate numbers of entry-level jobs would be available and that states and localities would act effectively to link former welfare recipients to those jobs. Meanwhile, budget surpluses encouraged even congressional Republicans to offer expensive new proposals.

My conclusion is simple: Even with the new constraints imposed by the Bush tax cut, it is now possible to think less defensively and more expansively about the role of the public sector in helping hard-pressed parents and families. Although the people remain generally mistrustful of government (particularly the federal government), Democrats and progressives have perhaps their best opportunity in a generation to offer sensible proposals rooted in the moral sentiments of working-class and middle-class Americans and addressed to the concrete needs of America's families.

A final framing point: While progressives remain unswerving in pursuit of historic ends, we must become more open-minded and innovative regarding means. Just as the British Labour Party finally recognized that public ownership of the means of production is not the best way of realizing the dreams of workers and their families, so U.S. Democrats and progressives must acknowledge that direct public provision of basic goods and services is not necessarily the best way of discharging public responsibility for broad access to these basics. If we have decided that food stamps rather than government supermarkets and food banks are the right way to eliminate hunger among low-income Americans, why can't we consider a resource-based strategy for housing or even (dare I say it) education?

TAX REFORM TO STRENGTHEN
MARRIAGE AND FAMILIES

The late 1940s witnessed the creation of a strongly profamily tax system. As a result, families at the median income with two children paid virtually no federal income taxes. While scholars disagree about the extent of the relation between economic incentives and family behavior, it is difficult to believe that the stability of marriage, explosion of child-bearing, and decline of divorce during the postwar years were unrelated to these developments in the law.

Over the past three decades, however, some basic features of the tax code shifted against the interests of married couples, especially two-earner couples with children. The real value of the personal exemption has been allowed to erode by nearly 75 percent since the 1950s. The ability of married couples to combine and then "split" their incomes, with each person taxed on his or her half directly, was effectively eliminated in 1969. Special provisions to compensate couples for the "marriage penalty" were curtailed. The tax code shifted in favor of single individuals, and the tax burden on median income families with children increased nearly tenfold. Here again, it is difficult to believe that adverse family trends since the 1960s are entirely unrelated to these changing incentives.[2]

In 1975, lawmakers came together across party lines to create the Earned Income Tax Credit, principally designed to supplement the incomes of low-income working families with dependent children. (A five-year, $21 billion increase in the EITC was the single largest social policy success in Bill Clinton's first term.) While the 1986 tax reform act virtually doubled the personal exemption, it totally eliminated provisions to counter the marriage penalty. The Clinton administration's successful effort in 1993 to increase the progressivity of the tax code had the unintended effect of exacerbating this penalty.

Although the 1997 tax bill did create a $500 per child tax credit, it also included numerous provisions that further increase the code's tilt against married couples. For example:

- Under this law, interest on student loans is deductible during the first five years that payments are required. But the deduction phases out for single incomes between $40,000 and $55,000, and for married incomes between $60,000 and $75,000. So two single college graduates who start work at $39,000/year can each deduct $1,000, for a total of $2,000; if they get married and have a joint income of $78,000, they get no deduction.
- The Roth individual retirement account allows tax-free withdrawals in retirement and permits holders of current IRAs to convert them to Roth accounts if their adjusted gross income (AGI) is under $100,000. So two singles each making $51,000 could convert without penalty; if they were married, they couldn't.
- In addition, single workers cannot contribute to Roth IRAs if their income exceeds $110,000; the ceiling for couples is $160,000. So singles making $80,000-$110,000 each could contribute, but not if they get married.
- Similar limits apply to contributions to IRAs for education expenses, with similar antimarriage consequences.
- The $500/child tax credit is reduced by $50 for each $1,000 that income exceeds $110,000 (for married couples) and $75,000 (for single heads of households). So if two singles, each making $70,000 and with one child, were to marry, their child tax credit would disappear.
- The law creates a special low capital gains rate of 10 percent for married persons up to about $41,000 annual income and singles up to about $25,000. So two singles with capital gains and incomes of $24,000 each would be taxed at 10 percent; if they married, their capital gains rate would double, to 20 percent.[3]

The prime source of the marriage penalty in the current tax code is the tension among three principles: progressivity; equal treatment of married couples with the same total earnings, regardless of the distribution of earnings between husband and wife; and marriage neutrality—the same tax treatment of individuals A and B, whether they are single or married.[4]

Box 1   A Marriage Penalty

A couple with $75,000 in total earnings, split evenly between the husband and the wife, would have incurred a marriage penalty of nearly $1,400 under 1996 tax law. The penalty results from two factors. First, the combined standard deduction for two individual tax filers would have been $8,000—$1,300 more than the standard deduction available on a joint return. At the couple's marginal tax rate of 28 percent, the lower deduction would have increased the couple's tax liability by $364 (28 percent of $1,300). Second, because tax brackets for joint returns were less than twice as wide as those for individual returns, $7,900 that is taxed at 15 percent on individual returns would have incurred a 28 percent rate on a joint return. That higher tax rate would have raised the couple's tax liability by an additional $1,027 (28 percent minus 15 percent equals 13 percent of $7,900). In combination, the two factors would have increased the couple's tax liability by 1.9 percent of their adjusted gross income.

	Husband	*Wife*	*Couple*
Adjusted Gross Income	$37,500	$37,500	$75,000
Less personal exemptions	2,550	2,550	5,100
Less standard deduction	4,000	4,000	6,700
Equals taxable income	30,950	30,950	63,200
Taxable at 15 percent	24,000	24,000	40,100
Taxable at 28 percent	6,950	6,950	23,100
Tax Liability	5,546	5,546	12,483
Marriage Penalty			$1,391
As a percent of Adjusted Gross Income			1.9

Source: Congressional Budget Office.

It turns out that there is no way of fulfilling these three principles simultaneously. For example, progressivity ensures that a couple in which each individual earns $37500 will pay more total taxes if they marry than if they remain single.

Note that these same structural principles can lead to marriage bonuses in cases in which one spouse earns all or most of the married couple's total income.

There are two ways of looking at this balance: static and dynamic. Under one standard static analysis, 42 percent of all married filers in 1996 experienced penalties, while 51 percent received bonuses and 6 percent were essentially unaffected. The average penalty was $1,380; the average bonus was

Box 2   A Marriage Bonus

A couple with $75,000 in total earnings, all earned by the wife, would have received a marriage bonus of nearly $4,000 under 1996 tax law. The bonus results from three factors. First, filing jointly, the couple would have claimed $5,100 in personal exemptions, twice what they could have claimed on two single returns. At a 31 percent tax rate, the larger exemption would have reduced the couple's tax liability by $791 (31 percent of $2,550). Second, the standard deduction of $6,700 on a joint return would have been $2,700 more than the $4,000 standard deduction the wife could have claimed on an individual return. (The husband, filing individually with no income, could not take the deduction.) At the couple's marginal tax rate of 31 percent, the larger deduction would have reduced the couple's tax liability by $837 (31 percent of $2,700). Finally, because tax brackets for joint returns were wider than those for individual returns, $16,100 that is taxed at 28 percent on individual returns would have been taxed at only 15 percent on a joint return and $5,050 taxed at 31 percent rather than at 28 percent. Those lower tax rates would have reduced the couple's tax liability by an additional $2,245 (28 percent minus 15 percent equals 13 percent of $16,100 plus 31 percent minus 28 percent equals 3 percent of $5,050). In combination, the three factors would have lowered the couple's tax liability by 5.2 percent of their adjusted gross income.

	Husband	Wife	Couple
Adjusted Gross Income	$0	$75,000	$75,000
Less personal exemptions	2,550	2,550	5,100
Less standard deduction	4,000	4,000	6,700
Equals taxable income	0	68,450	63,200
Taxable at 15 percent	0	24,000	40,100
Taxable at 28 percent	0	34,150	23,100
Taxable at 31 percent	0	10,300	0
Tax Liability	0	16,355	12,483
Marriage Bonus			$3,872
As a percent of Adjusted Gross Income			15.2

Source: Congressional Budget Office.

slightly less ($1,300); and the tax code awarded an overall marriage bonus of about $4 billion ($33 billion in bonuses minus $29 billion in penalties).

So it is too simple to say that our current tax code is comprehensively biased against marriage. Rather, it tilts against certain kinds of marriages—namely, those in which husbands and wives are both in the paid workforce earning the same or similar salaries. This remains the case even after the modest reductions in the marriage penalty enacted as part of the 2001 tax bill.

A dynamic analysis suggests a different picture. Between 1969 and 1995, the share of all married couples in which both spouses worked outside the home increased from 46 to 60 percent, while the proportion with just one worker fell from 46 to 25 percent. The increase for married couples with children was particularly sharp: from 54 to 74 percent for couples with one child, and from 33 to 67 percent for couples with two or more children. In 1969, only 17 percent of working-age married couples were characterized by rough equality of earnings between husband and wife (the technical definition: each spouse contributes at least one-third of the couple's total earnings). By 1995, that percentage had doubled, to about 34 percent. This statistic suggests that if all other variables had remained constant, the percentage of couples experiencing marriage penalties would have increased sharply between 1969 and 1995. To put it the other way around: if the demographic profile of married couples had not changed over the past quarter century, two-thirds of couples would get marriage bonuses (versus today's actual figure of about one-half) and fewer than one-third would pay penalties (versus today's actual figure of about two-fifths).

Based on this history, the case for tax reform to promote the interests of contemporary married couples appears strong. Let me suggest a few principles that might guide this effort.

1. The tax code should not create a substantial group of married taxpayers that is worse off than its members would be if they were unmarried.
2. There should be no bias in the tax code for or against work in the household economy.
3. There should be no bias in the tax code against the decision to have children. As a related issue, the code should embody a social recognition of the internalized family costs and external public benefits of childrearing.
4. There should be no substantial group of married taxpayers that would be worse off under reform proposals than under the status quo.

Joint versus separate taxation

As we debate the reduction or elimination of the marriage penalty, the American people and their representatives should discuss these principles in some detail—especially the fourth, because it screens out options that many might find appealing. For example, 19 out of 27 countries in the OECD impose income taxes separately on the earnings of husbands and wives. (Only 3 other OECD nations have embraced the U.S. strategy of joint taxation.) For all practical purposes, separate taxation eliminates the effect of marriage on a couple's taxes (fulfilling the criterion of marriage neutrality discussed previously), while violating the criterion of equal tax treatment for couples with the same total incomes.

Prior to 1948, the United States employed separate taxation. The movement to joint taxation in that year was defended as promarriage. And in the context of a social structure dominated by single-earner households, it was. But today, joint taxation divides married couples into winners ("traditional" households with a single dominant earner) and losers (modern two-earner households with two significant contributors to total family incomes). Restoring and mandating individual filing would be roughly revenue-neutral (it would increase federal revenues by a modest $4 billion annually) and would eliminate the marriage penalty for the nearly 21 million couples now incurring them. But it would also increase taxes by an average of $1,300 for the 25 million couples enjoying marriage bonuses under the current system.

By themselves, these raw numbers would constitute a formidable political barrier to change. To complicate matters further, the tax increases would fall disproportionately on couples where one spouse has made the decision to remain at home to care for young children, exacerbating the perception of an economic and cultural bias against the home economy.

The alternative is to hold all married couples harmless by allowing them to choose between filing jointly or separately. Assuming that each couple made the economically rational choice, this approach would reduce annual federal revenues by an estimated $29 billion—roughly the value of all marriage penalties in the existing code. It is not unreasonable to wonder whether the social benefits of this approach are commensurate with its hefty price tag.

Reforming the Earned Income Tax Credit (EITC)

The tension among the principles of progressivity, equal treatment of equal family incomes, and marriage neutrality operates with special intensity on the EITC. Consider the choice faced by two low-wage earners, each an EITC recipient with one child. With a family income of $22,000, the marriage penalty is $3,700, a staggering 17 percent of adjusted gross income.

This may seem like a somewhat atypical case; after all, relatively few single men have sole responsibility for children. So let's vary it slightly: Assume that the man is a childless minimum wage worker, while the woman is a former AFDC recipient with two children.

The EITC rewards work, fights poverty, and promotes tax fairness. But while it is one of the most morally admirable portions of our tax code, it is also the principal source of the marriage penalty for low-income couples. Removing this penalty is neither cheap nor straightforward, however, as a recent study by the Congressional Budget Office makes clear.

Box 3   A Marriage Penalty for a Low-Income Couple with Children

A couple with two children and $22,000 in total earnings, split evenly between the husband and wife, would have incurred a marriage penalty of $3,701 under 1996 tax law. The penalty results from two factors. First, if they were not married, both the husband and the wife could file as heads of household, each claiming one child as a dependent. As heads of household, their combined standard deductions would have been $11,800, $5,100 more than the $6,700 standard deduction available on a joint return. At the couple's marginal tax rate of 15 percent, the lower deduction would have increased the couple's tax liability by $765 (15 percent of $5,100). Second, filing separate returns, the husband and wife each could have claimed the maximum earned income tax credit (EITC) for a filer with one child, $2,152. Filing jointly, the couple would have received only one, smaller EITC of $1,368. Thus, filing jointly the couple would have received a payment of $603, about $3,700 less than the $4,304 they would have gotten if they could have filed separately.

	Husband	Wife	Couple
Adjusted Gross Income	$11,000	$11,000	$22,000
Less personal exemptions	5,100	5,100	10,200
Less standard deduction	5,900	5,900	6,700
Equals taxable income	0	0	5,100
Tax (at 15 percent)	0	0	765
Less earned income as tax credit	2,152	2,152	1,368
Tax Liability	-2,152	-2,152	-603
Marriage Penalty			$3,701
As a percent of Adjusted Gross Income			16.8

Source: Congressional Budget Office.
' Baseline for calculating marriage penalty assumes that both husband and wife file as head of household with one child.

One option analyzed by the CBO would totally eliminate the penalty by allowing each parent to receive the EITC on the basis of his or her individual income. This approach would have a number of negative or counterintuitive consequences. For example, it would remove all limits on the total combined income of families receiving the credit, and it would expand the number of recipient families by more than 11 million—many at the upper end of the income spectrum. (A model case: the husband makes $60,000 and the wife, $10,000. Under existing family income limits, these taxpayers would not be eligible for the EITC; under the individual income option, the wife would receive payments.) In addition, the CBO estimates the overall annual cost (lost revenues plus increased outlays) of this approach at about $14 billion.

A second option, with an annual price tag of roughly $10 billion, would preserve the current family basis of the EITC while setting income eligibility limits for couples at twice the levels for individuals. (The current cutoff, which applies to both individuals and couples, is $28,495; the new cutoff for married couples would be almost $57,000.) Ninety percent of the benefits under this approach would go to couples making less than $50,000, and it would eliminate the marriage penalty for the family discussed earlier with two earners at the minimum wage. Still, it seems more than a bit odd to allow families with incomes almost 50 percent above the national median to qualify for a program intended to benefit the working poor.

A third option, which would make an additional 3.7 million couples eligible for the EITC and cost about $4 billion per year, requires spouses to pool and split their earnings and then allows them to qualify for the EITC as individuals. Like the second option, this approach would resolve the problems faced by the dual minimum-wage family. In contrast to the second option, it would mean lower payments for some couples—those in which one spouse earns substantially more than the other. Virtually all the benefits would go to families with incomes below $50,000 who are now experiencing marriage penalties.

Dependent exemptions and credits

During the 1950s, at the peak of the family-friendly tax code, married couples with two children at the median income paid federal income taxes at an effective rate of 5.6 percent, versus about 9 percent in the early 1990s. Similar families at half the median income (the working poor) paid no federal income taxes whatever, compared to an effective rate of about 5 percent by the early 1990s. The principal cause of these shifts is not higher marginal tax rates (which are in fact lower than they were forty years ago), but rather a decline in the value of the dependent exemption, in real inflation-adjusted terms and as a percentage of median income.

A rough calculation indicates that restoring the value of the dependent exemption to the level of the 1950s would require a dependent exemption of at least $8,000; the actual figure today is about $2,300. But this overstates the size of the problem. The $500 per child tax credit enacted in 1997 is the equivalent of an increase of $3,300 in the dependent exemption for working-class families in the 15 percent bracket and $1,800 for middle-class families in the 28 percent bracket. So working-class families now enjoy dependents' tax benefits totaling $5,600 (2,300 + 3,300) per dependent, while the total for middle-class families is $4,100 (2,300 + 1,800).

This simple calculation shows that an additional $500 credit per child (above and beyond what was done in 1997) would just about bring families with dependents back to where they were forty years ago. This strategy would be especially effective if the credit were targeted to lower- and middle-income families and made applicable to payroll as well as income taxes. For example, a low-income family with two children may not pay $1,000 in federal income taxes but would receive the full $1,000 credit, a portion of which would in effect reduce its payroll tax burden. The child credit provisions of the 2001 tax act move some distance in this direction.

Payroll taxes

For many families with dependent children, the increase in the federal income tax has been dwarfed by increases in the payroll tax. In the mid-1950s, working-class families paid payroll taxes at the rate of 4.0 percent, and middle-class families at 3.4 percent, versus 15.3 today. Even upper-middle-class families, much of whose income is excluded from the Social Security taxable base, have experienced major increases (table 1).

Given these trends, it is reasonable to look for ways of reducing the payroll tax burden for families with dependent children. The difficulty, of course, is that these efforts take place against the backdrop of projected long-term financing problems for the Social Security system and increasing political challenges to the program in its current form.

There are three basic strategies available for reducing families' payroll tax burdens: (1) increasing the payroll tax for other workers; (2) shifting some of the financing to general revenues; or (3) not compensating for revenue losses, further increasing the long-term financial pressures on the Social Security system. In my judgment, strategy 3 is substantively irresponsible and a political nonstarter. Strategy 2 is unwise to the extent that it weakens the moral basis of the system—namely, retirement benefits in return for (though not in proportion to) contributions during one's working life. By process of elimination, strategy 1 emerges as the most promising, though hardly free of difficulty.

What could be done? One possibility would be to reduce the employee portion of the payroll tax by, say, 1.5 percent per dependent child. A working-class family with two children at half the median income would see its payroll taxes cut by about $600 a year; families at the median income would see an annual cut of roughly $1,200. (This would roll back payroll taxes for these families to roughly the levels that prevailed in 1980.) Another possibility in the same vein would be to exempt from the Social Security tax base an amount equal to the value of the dependent deduction ($2,300) multiplied by the number of dependents. A very rough calculation suggests an annual revenue loss of roughly $25-30 billion; compensating for it would require a significant payroll tax increase for all workers without dependent children.

Table 1. Federal Income and Payroll Taxes as a Share of Family Income, 1955–1991

	Half Median Income			Median Income			Twice Median Income		
Year	Federal Income Tax	Social Security Tax	Total	Federal Income Tax	Social Security Tax	Total	Federal Income Tax	Social Security Tax	Total
1955	0.0	4.0	4.0	5.6	3.4	9.1	10.8	1.7	12.5
1960	0.2	6.0	6.2	7.8	4.6	12.4	12.1	2.3	14.4
1965	2.2	7.3	9.4	7.1	4.5	11.6	11.1	2.2	13.4
1970	4.7	9.6	14.3	9.4	6.7	16.1	13.5	3.4	16.8
1975	4.2	11.7	15.9	9.6	10.4	20.0	14.9	5.2	20.1
1980	6.0	12.3	18.3	11.4	12.3	23.7	18.3	6.5	24.8
1985	6.6	14.1	20.7	10.3	14.1	24.4	16.8	8.5	25.3
1990	5.1	15.3	20.3	9.3	15.3	24.6	15.1	9.5	24.6
1991	4.8	15.3	20.1	9.2	15.3	24.5	15.0	10.6	25.6

Source: C. Eugene and Ion M. Bakija, *Retooling Social Security for the 21st Century: Right and Wrong Approaches to Reform* (Washington, DC: Urban Institute Press, 1994), 160. Original Sources: U.S. Department of Treasury Office of Tax Analysis (Allen Lerman), U.S. Bureau Current Population Reports (various issues), U.S. Internal Revenue Service Statistics of Income (various issues), and authors' calculations.

A very different strategy would avoid the need to shift tax burdens among classes of workers, focusing instead on ways of allowing workers to shift burdens and benefits from one period of their lives to another. So, for example, workers who take advantage of the payroll tax reduction for minor children might be required to pay higher rates for the remainder of their working lives after their children are grown. Conversely, it might be possible to allow young workers to draw from their Social Security accounts for some family-related purposes (e.g., financing an extended leave from the paid workforce after the birth of a child). This would require these workers to choose between higher tax rates later on and retirement benefits that are actuarially reduced by the value (principal plus interest over time) of the funds withdrawn.

A wild new idea

Consider a thought experiment comparing two stylized societies. In society A, virtually every couple is married, but no marriage lasts for more than a few years. (There is a very high rate of divorce and remarriage.) In society B, only half of the adults ever marry, but every marriage lasts until the death of a spouse. I don't know of many people who would consider society A to be a model for families and childrearing. Most people who care about these things probably want a society that combines the high marriage rate of A with the stability of B. But my guess is that if forced to choose, most of these people would opt for B. If this is right (every reader will have to run the thought experiment for him- or herself), it reveals a significant fact: our interest in the stability of marital relations exceeds our concern for the statistical incidence of couples in the legal category of marriage.

Suppose we wanted to create a tax code that encouraged and rewarded marital stability rather than just status. What would we do? Here's a blue-sky proposal: after five years of marriage, begin reducing a couple's overall taxes by 1 percent a year for each subsequent year, up to a maximum of (say) thirty years. So, for example, a couple married for fifteen years would calculate its gross taxes for that year and then reduce that figure by 10 percent (fifteen years minus the base of five years multiplied by 1 percent/year). Couples married for thirty years or more would experience a tax reduction of 25 percent. My hunch is that these numbers are big enough to serve as a significant disincentive to divorce in a large number of cases.

HOUSING

The story of public housing assistance over the past three decades is not a happy one. The oldest and best known form of assistance is publicly owned and operated housing, initially authorized by the Housing Act of 1937. While quantitatively disappointing (only 1.2 million units have been produced during the past sixty years), this program still works reasonably well in some areas. In many central cities, however, the quality of this housing (typically, though not invariably, high-rise apartments) has declined dramatically, crime has surged in and around the buildings, and working class married couples have been squeezed out in favor of the extreme poor—typically, single mothers with minor children. The physical deterioration was so severe, that in 1996 the Department of Housing and Urban Development established a goal of demolishing 100,000 of the worst units by the year 2000. In several cities, including Washington, DC, pervasive management failures prompted federal takeovers.

Still, there is a huge waiting list (estimated at 1 million families nationally), suggesting that for many poor people this housing represents the best available combination of quality and price. Recent efforts to improve public housing include enhanced security, expedited eviction procedures for drug dealers and other offenders, and the relaxation of strict income eligibility limits to increase the percentage of married and employed tenants.

Other housing programs—notably, subsidies to private developers to stimulate the creation of low-income housing, direct assistance to tenants, and efforts to promote the "deconcentration" of the poor—have been more successful. But many of these programs have proved vulnerable to political manipulation and scandal, and some of the most highly touted efforts (for example, the conversion of public housing to private ownership) have involved unsustainably high costs per beneficiary.

Most experts agree that the core housing problem for low-income people is not availability but rather affordability. This suggests that programs focused on the supply side needlessly divert resources from the intended beneficiaries to private developers and building managers. It is also widely agreed that the expansion of ownership (as opposed to renting) creates significant advantages for both individuals and communities.[5]

What would we do if we were able to mobilize the resources to realize the National Housing Goal, promulgated by Congress nearly fifty years ago, of a "decent [affordable] home and suitable living environment for every American family"? The following proposals are intentionally unconstrained by political and fiscal realities.

To begin, we would establish as an entitlement a housing voucher keyed to income and family size. The voucher's purpose would be to fill the gap between median housing costs (around $600 per month) and 30 percent of family cash income, defined as the sum of earned income and EITC payments.[6] (thirty percent of income is the affordability standard used by most existing

HUD programs.) So, for example, a family with two children and gross earned income of $11,000 now receives an annual EITC payment of $3,560, for a total cash income of $14,560. Thirty percent of that total is $4,368, or $364 per month. So the family would be eligible for a monthly voucher worth $236 ($600 minus $364)—an annual housing subsidy of $2,832. To avoid large transfers to nonworking families (and to increase work incentives for very low-income individuals), no family's housing voucher would be allowed to exceed its EITC payment. And because the lion's share of the EITC goes to families with children (the annual maximum for childless individuals is only $323 and payments phase out altogether when annual income reaches $9,500), the housing voucher would principally benefit parents and their dependents.

I don't have a very precise estimate of the cost of this proposal. But note that the housing voucher phases out entirely for families with incomes above $24,000, which is almost $4,500 less than the EITC cutoff. So because fewer families would be eligible for the voucher than for the EITC and each family's voucher would be capped at the EITC amount, the total cost of the program would be somewhat less than the EITC, which now has annual outlays of about $25 billion. (To provide some sense of relative size: annual federal support for low-income housing is less than $10 billion; the annual cost of the mortgage interest deduction is $66 billion.)

If home ownership is an important policy goal, there would be no reason to limit the use of the voucher to rental expenses. Recipients would be allowed to combine it with other income sources to qualify for home mortgages and meet monthly payments. The federal government could reinforce the push toward increased home ownership by transferring its inventory of single-family homes to local public housing authorities or community development corporations for quick resale and by supporting community-based groups, such as the Industrial Areas Foundation, that forge effective housing partnerships with the public, private, and voluntary sectors. And to help families that can afford monthly mortgage payments but cannot scrape together funds for down payments and closing costs, the government could create a fund for loans that would be secured by equity in homes and recovered with interest from proceeds at the time of resale.[7]

One possibility for financing these and related housing proposals would be to shift the structure of the mortgage interest deduction in a more progressive direction. At present, taxpayers are not allowed to deduct interest payments for the portion of their mortgage that exceeds $1 million. One straightforward proposal is to lower this cap to (say) $250,000. An alternative would be to directly limit the amount of interest deductible annually to (say) $20,000, an amount roughly equivalent to annual interest costs on a home mortgage of

$250,000 at current interest rates. The latter proposal, unlike the former, would leave borrowers exposed to nondeductible interest costs when interest rates rise significantly.

SUMMARY: PUBLIC POLICY, FAMILY INCOME, AND WAGES

Enacting the principal proposals discussed thus far—reducing the marriage penalty, doubling the $500 per child tax credit while applying it to payroll as well as income taxes, lowering payroll taxes for workers with minor children, and instituting a housing credit keyed to family income and the EITC—would increase the disposable incomes of working-class and middle-class families with dependent children by thousands of dollars annually. But these public policy instruments do little to affect underlying patterns of income derived from work.

Over the past decade, median family income rose from $46,344 to $49,940. Married couples did better, increasing from $51,922 to $56,827. Female-headed families lagged far behind, with median incomes rising from $23,163 to $26,164.[8]

Despite the tight labor markets and across-the-board wage gains in recent years, the long-term trend remains one of wage stagnation in the middle, sharp drops at the bottom, and even sharper increases at the top. I subscribe to the conventional explanation that globalization has reduced the ability of key players—business, organized labor, and government—to maintain the terms of the social contract that characterized the quarter century after World War II. Still, there are some strategies that should be tried:

1. The ability of workers to organize should not be impeded by antiquated or unenforced labor laws.
2. Someone should announce a new moral norm of compensation: chief executive officers of firms shouldn't make more than (say) one hundred times the wages of their lowest-paid workers. The names of the firms and CEOs that violate this norm should be publicized regularly, and the offenders should be asked to justify their conduct. (Responses that simply invoke "the free market" would receive a grade of F.)
3. Another norm, which might be reinforced through the tax code (although I'm not sure just how): compensation options available to top officials in a firm should be available to all employees as well. So if CEOs can receive stock options and profit-sharing plans, everyone should. In a period in which profits and stock prices are increasing faster than base wages, a

strategy of "universal gain-sharing" offers the best hope for increasing the total compensation of average workers.

Having said this, I incline to the contrarian view that the role of government in leaning against rising market-induced inequality will increase rather than decrease over the next generation. But efforts to discharge this responsibility through measures that restrain market competition (e.g., restrictive international trade agreements, new regulations on domestic business activities) are not likely to succeed. Rather, government will have to act directly to reduce inequality and increase opportunity. I call this the "progressive market strategy." The EITC, child tax credit, and proposed housing credit are all examples of policies consistent with this strategy. In the next decade, we will have to work harder, intellectually and politically, to find ways in which government can act to compensate the sectors of society that are harmed by global competition and to make the sources of upward mobility in the new economy available to all.

In a spirit of speculative adventure, let me sketch two largish policy concepts under the "progressive market" rubric. (I'm not sure of the merits or practicalities of either one, but they strike me as being worthy of discussion.)

Wage insurance

When I was serving in the Clinton administration, I tried without much success to promote discussion of a plan for "wage insurance." The basic idea was straightforward: in the new economy, pressures from technology, trade, and other factors are producing downward pressures on wages. Many individuals who lose high-paying jobs discover that their next job will pay significantly less and that it will take several years (sometimes longer) to struggle back to prior levels of compensation. In the new economy, in short, wage loss is a problem independent of unemployment. The old model of cyclical unemployment, to which unemployment insurance (UI) was a reasonable policy response, must now be modified to include the risk of noncyclical wage loss, about which the current UI system does nothing.

That raises an obvious question: Would it be possible in principle to design a system of wage insurance that builds on the UI system? The answer, I believe, is yes. Imagine a contributory system into which all workers pay, say, one-half of 1 percent of their wage income, generating a trust fund of (depending on the details) $10-20 billion annually. Workers who experience involuntary wage losses would be eligible for insurance compensation of, say, half their losses for a period of three years or until they recover their previous wage levels (whichever comes first).[9] Translating this concept into a workable program would not be easy. We would have to answer detailed questions about eligibility criteria, actuarial soundness, and administerability, among others. But the idea should be sustained by its underlying moral power: the distribution of benefits and burdens in the new economy is highly uneven, and many of us are exposed to risks that are hard to anticipate and mitigate under current circumstances.

Wage insurance represents meaningful recognition of the fact that we're all in it together and that those of us who are gaining from changes in technology and patterns of competition have a responsibility to share our gains with those who aren't.

Wage subsidies

Columbia University's Edmund Phelps has proposed a bold plan for increasing wages flowing to low-wage labor. Under his plan, firms would be subsidized for hiring low-wage workers on a sliding scale that would phase out at $12 per hour. Although some portion of this subsidy would go to the firm, much of it would help bid up the price of low-wage labor while dramatically reducing unemployment among lower-skilled workers.

The gross cost of this program would be enormous—on the order of $100 billion per year. Its net cost would be significantly lower, perhaps only half the gross: it would replace the EITC (currently $35 billion/year) and reduce costs for programs such as Medicaid, food stamps, and TANF (the successor to AFDC). But most important, it would improve the attractiveness to employers of potential workers now at the end of the labor market queue. And it could "make work pay" for young people now living in communities where alternatives to legal employment have proved so appealing. If Phelps is right, this will also increase incentives for these potential workers to obtain the education and job skills they need to succeed in the new economy, and it could also increase the propensity of employers to invest in these workers, who are now overlooked in most workplace-based training programs.[10]

NOTES

1. Theda Skocpol, "A Partnership with American Families," in *The New Majority: Toward a Popular Progressive Politics*, ed. Stanley B. Greenberg and Theda Skocpol (New Haven: Yale University Press, 1997), 123.

2. For more detail on this sad history, see Elaine Ciulla Kamarck and William A. Galston, "A Progressive Family Policy for the 1990s," in *Mandate for Change*, ed. Will Marshall and Martin Schram (New York: Berkley Books, 1993).

3. See Albert B. Crenshaw, "For Two-Income Couples, More Reasons Not to Get Tied," *Washington Post*, August 24, 1997, Hl.

4. See "For Better or for Worse: Marriage and the Federal Income Tax" (Congressional Budget Office, June 1997), 3. This careful study is the source for most of the statistics in this section of my chapter.

5. See Chester W. Hartman, "Memo to the Social Science Research Council Regarding U.S. Housing Policy," prepared for the SSRC's Committee for Research on the Urban Underclass, October 1993.

6. For a useful summary of federal home ownership strategies, see "Moving Up to the American Dream: From Public Housing to Private Homeownership" (U.S. Department of Housing and Urban Development, July 1996).

7. *Money Income in the United States*, 1999 (U.S. Census Bureau P60-209, September 2000), x.

8. I note with interest that Robert Z. Lawrence and Robert E. Litan have suggested something along these lines in a Brookings "Policy Brief" (September 1997, no. 24).

9. Edmund Phelps, *Rewarding Work* (Cambridge: Harvard University Press, 1997). My comments are based on summaries by Alan Wolfe, "The Moral Meanings of Work," *The American Prospect* (September/October 1997): 87; and the staff of the *Economist* (September 20-26, 1997), 47.

10. Ibid.

Part III

RELIGION

Chapter Nine

Conscience, Religious Accommodation, and Political Authority (2003)

In a modern welfare state, such as the United States, most aspects of life are exposed to laws and regulations. Often these authoritative public pronouncements have the effect of restricting the free exercise of religion. This in turn gives rise to demands that the state "accommodate" religion by refraining from enforcing on the affected believers commands or prohibitions binding on other citizens.

Since the end of World War II, the response of the U.S. Supreme Court to these demands has gone through two distinct phases. In the first, the Court defined a regime of required accommodations: if a state action pursuing a generally valid public purpose has the effect of significantly burdening religious free exercise, then the state must show both that the public interests at stake are "compelling" and that its action has been carefully designed to minimize the intrusion on religious practice. If not, then religiously motivated requests for exemptions from the full force of the law enjoy at least presumptive validity.

In 1990, however, in the case of *Employment Division v. Smith*, the Court turned this regime on its head, deciding that the state of Oregon was not required to exempt Native Americans who use peyote in their religious ceremonies from the requirements of its drug laws. Writing for the majority, Justice Antonin Scalia argued that many laws would fail the compelling state interest test. "Any society adopting such a system," he declared, "would be courting anarchy, but that danger increase in direct proportion to the society's diversity of religious beliefs, and its determination to coerce or suppress none of them." He concluded that "we cannot afford the luxury of deeming *presumptively invalid*, as applied to the religious objector, every regulation that does not protect an interest of the highest order. . . . [Such a rule] would open the prospect of constitutionally required

111

religious exemptions from civic obligations of almost every kind." The *Smith* decision produced an outraged backlash across a wide range of religious denominations and led to the passage in 1993 of the Religious Freedom Restoration Act, which the Court subsequently nullified.

FREEDOM OF CONSCIENCE: TWO CASES

Justice Scalia's line of argument struck many observers as wholly unexpected and unprecedented, a legal bolt from the blue. In fact, it drew on an important but largely forgotten episode in U.S. constitutional history. I begin my tale in the late 1930s.

Acting under the authority of the state government, the school board of Minersville, Pennsylvania, had required both students and teachers to participate in a daily pledge of allegiance to the flag. In the 1940 case of *Minersville v. Gobitis*, the Supreme Court decided against a handful of Jehovah's Witnesses who sought to have their children exempted on the grounds that this exercise amounted to a form of idolatry strictly forbidden by their faith. With but a single dissenting vote, the Court ruled that it was permissible for a school board to make participation in saluting the American flag a condition for attending public school, regardless of the conscientious objections of parents and students. Nearly half a century later, Justice Scalia cited the key passage from the majority decision in *Gobitis*, written by Felix Frankfurter, to bolster his controversial holding in *Smith*.

But this historical drama has a second act. Quoting liberally from Frankfurter's *Gobitis* decision, the West Virginia State Board of Education quickly issued a regulation making the flag salute mandatory statewide. When a challenge to this action arose barely three years after *Gobitis*, the Court reversed itself, in *West Virginia v. Barnette*, by a vote of 6 to 3. To be sure, during the brief interval separating these cases, the lone dissenter in *Gobitis* had been elevated to Chief Justice and two new voices, both favoring reversal, had joined the court, while two supporters of the original decision had departed. But of the seven justices who heard both cases, three saw fit to reverse themselves and to set forth their reasons for the change.

This kind of abrupt, explicit reversal is very rare in the annals of the Court, and it calls for some explanation. A clue is to be found, I believe, in the well-known peroration of Justice Robert Jackson's majority decision overturning compulsory flag salutes:

> If there is any fixed star in our constitutional constellation, it is that no official, high or petty, can prescribe what shall be orthodox in politics, nationalism, reli-

gion, or other matters of opinion or force citizens to confess by word or act their faith therein. If there are any circumstances which permit an exception, they do not now occur to us. We think the action of the local authorities in compelling the flag salute and pledge transcends constitutional limitation on their power and invades the sphere of intellect and spirit which it is the purpose of the First Amendment to our Constitution to reserve from all official control.

I want to suggest that the protected "sphere of intellect and spirit" to which Jackson refers enjoys a central place in the development of American law and culture, and in liberal democratic theory more generally.

SUBSTANTIVE DUE PROCESS, FUNDAMENTAL LIBERTIES, AND FREEDOM OF CONSCIENCE

In the century after the adoption of the Constitution, the Supreme Court played at most a minor role in protecting what we now understand as the basic civil rights of individuals. During the decades after the Civil War, the Court increasingly deployed a broad construction of individual property rights against the states while typically leaving political and civil liberties under the aegis of state power, a jurisprudential strategy that reached its peak in the famous (for some, infamous) 1905 decision of *Lochner v. New York*. Legal commentators and dissenting justices began asking how these two tendencies could be reconciled.

In 1920, for example, the case of *Gilbert v. Minnesota* came before the Supreme Court. Gilbert, a pacifist, had criticized American participation in World War I. He was convicted under a state statute prohibiting advocacy or teaching that interfered with or discouraged enlistment in the military. While the Court's majority declined to extend Fourteenth Amendment liberty guarantees to Gilbert, Justice Brandeis dissented, writing:

I have difficulty believing that the liberty guaranteed by the Constitution, which has been held to protect [a wide property right], does not include liberty to teach, either in the privacy of the home or publicly, the doctrine of pacifism . . . I cannot believe that the liberty guaranteed by the 14th Amendment includes only liberty to acquire and to enjoy property.

Over time, the Court's unwillingness to abandon its doctrine of broad economic rights helped create the basis for a broader understanding of constitutionally protected and enforceable liberties. Two important cases decided in the 1920s spearheaded this expansion and helped lay the foundation for nationally recognized rights of conscience. The first stemmed from a Nebraska law which, reflecting the nativist passions stirred by World War One, prohibited instruction in any modern language other than English. Acting under this statute, a trial court convicted a teacher in a Lutheran parochial school for teaching a Bible class in German. In *Meyer v. Nebraska* (1923), the Supreme Court struck down this law as a violation of the Fourteenth Amendment's liberty guarantee. Writing for a seven-member majority, Justice McReynolds declared:

> That the State may do much, go very far, indeed, in order to improve the quality of its citizens, physically, mentally, and morally, is clear; but the individual has certain fundamental rights which must be respected. A desirable end cannot be promoted by prohibited means.

Two years later, the Supreme Court handed down a second key ruling. The background to the case was this: through a ballot initiative, the people of Oregon enacted a law requiring all parents and legal guardians to send children between the ages of eight and sixteen to public schools. This amounted to outlawing most non-public schools. The Society of Sisters, an Oregon corporation that maintained a system of Catholic schools, sued on the grounds that this law was inconsistent with the Fourteenth Amendment. In *Pierce v. Society of Sisters*, decided in 1925, the Court agreed. Justice McReynolds, this time writing for a unanimous court, declared:

> The fundamental theory of liberty upon which all governments in this Union repose excludes any general power of the State to standardize its children by forcing them to accept instruction from public teachers only. The child is not the mere creature of the State . . .

I now jump forward six years, to 1931. In that year, the Supreme Court handed down its decision in the case of *U.S. v. Macintosh*. The facts were as follows: Douglas Clyde Macintosh was born in Canada, came to the U.S. as a graduate student at the University of Chicago, and was ordained as a Baptist minister in 1907. He began teaching at Yale in 1909 and in short order became a member of the faculty of the Divinity school, Chaplain of the Yale Graduate School, and Dwight Professor of Theology. When World War I broke out, he returned to his native Canada and volunteered for service on the front as a military chaplain. He reentered the U.S. in 1916 and applied for naturalization in 1925. When asked whether he would bear arms on behalf of his country, he said he would not give a blanket undertaking in advance without knowing the cause for which his country was asking him to fight or believing that the war was just, declaring that "his first allegiance was to the will of God." After he was denied naturalization, he went to court.

The government argued that naturalization was a privilege, not a right, that the government has the right to impose any conditions it sees fit on that privilege, that the exemption of native-born citizens from military service on grounds of conscience was a statutory grant, not a Constitutional right, and that the Congress had not provided such statutory exemption for individuals seeking naturalization. The lawyers for Macintosh argued that our history makes it clear that conscientious exemption from military service was an integral element of the rights of conscience, guaranteed by the First Amendment, that inhere in individuals and that in any event this was one of the rights reserved to the people by the Ninth Amendment.

By a vote of 5 to 4, a deeply divided Court decided in favor of the government. The case turned both on matters of statutory construction and on broader considerations. Writing for the majority, Justice Sutherland said:

> When [Macintosh] speaks of putting his allegiance to the will of God above his allegiance to the government, it is evident, in light of his entire statement that he means to make his own interpretation of the will of God the decisive test which shall conclude the government and stay its hand. We are a Christian people . . . according to one another the equal right of religious freedom, and acknowledging with reverence the duty of obedience to the will of God. But, also, we are a Nation with the duty to survive; a Nation whose Constitution contemplates war as well as peace; whose government must go forward upon the assumption, and safely can proceed upon no other, that qualified obedience to the Nation and submission and obedience to the laws of the land, as well those made for war as those made for peace, are not inconsistent with the will of God.

Writing for the four dissenters, Chief Justice Hughes began by offering an argument based on statutory construction, but like Sutherland, he did not end there. Hughes framed the broader argument this way:

> Much has been said of the paramount duty to the State, a duty to be recognized, it is urged, even though it conflicts with convictions of duty to God. Undoubtedly that duty to the State exists within the domain of power, for government may enforce obedience to laws regardless of scruples. When one's belief collides with the power of the State, the latter is supreme within its sphere and submission or punishment follows. But, in the forum of conscience, duty to a moral power higher than the State has always been maintained. The reservation of that supreme obligation, as a matter of principle, would undoubtedly be made by many of our conscientious and law-abiding citizens. The essence of religion is belief in a relation to God involving duties superior to those arising from any human relation . . . . One cannot speak of religious liberty, with proper appreciation of its essential and historic significance, without assuming the existence of a belief in supreme allegiance to the will of God. . . . [F]reedom of conscience

itself implies respect for an innate conviction of paramount duty. The battle for religious liberty has been fought and won with respect to religious beliefs and practices, which are not in conflict with good order, upon the very ground of the supremacy of conscience within its proper field. What that field is, under our system of government, presents in part a question of constitutional law and also, in part, one of legislative policy in avoiding unnecessary clashes with the dictates of conscience. There is abundant room for enforcing the requisite authority of law as it is enacted and requires obedience, and for maintaining the conception of the supremacy of law as essential to orderly government, without demanding that either citizens or applicants for citizenship shall assume by oath an obligation to regard allegiance to God as subordinate to allegiance to civil power.

FROM *GOBITIS* TO *BARNETTE*: THE RISE AND FALL OF FELIX FRANKFURTER

This brings us to the dueling court decisions sketched earlier. Writing for the majority in *Minersville v. Gobitis*, Justice Frankfurter offered an argument in favor of a democratic state whose legitimate powers include the power to prescribe civic exercises such as the flag salute. He began by locating the controversy in a complex field of plural and competing claims: liberty of individual conscience versus the state's authority to safeguard the nation's civic unity. The task is to "reconcile" these competing claims, which means "prevent[ing] either from destroying the other." Because liberty of conscience is so fundamental, "every possible leeway" should be given to the claims of religious faith. Still, Frankfurter reasoned, the "very plurality of principles" prevents us from establishing the "freedom to follow conscience" as absolute.

Frankfurt's thesis that the free exercise of conscience is inherently limited was squarely in the jurisprudential mainstream. In a line of cases extending back to 1878, the Supreme Court had distinguished between religious belief, which enjoys total immunity from state action, and religious practices, which may be regulated or even prohibited if they run afoul of basic individual or social interests that government has a duty to protect. In *Cantwell v. Connecticut*, decided just weeks before *Gobitis*, the Court expounded this distinction with exceptional clarity:

> The religion clause of the First Amendment embraces two concepts—freedom to believe and freedom to act. The first is absolute but, in the nature of things, the second cannot be. Conduct remains subject to regulation for the protection of society. The freedom to act must have appropriate definition to preserve the enforcement of that protection. In every case the power to regulate must be so exercised as not, in attaining a permissible end, unduly to infringe the protected freedom.

Frankfurter turned next to the meaning of the clashing principles of political and religious authority. He suggested that in considering the judicial enforcement of religious freedom we are dealing with a "historic concept." That is, we should not look at its underlying logic or principles, but rather and only at the way this concept has been applied in the past. He asserted that "conscientious scruples have not, in the course of the long struggle for religious toleration, relieved the individual from obedience to a general law not aimed at the promotion or restriction of religious belief. . . . The mere possession of religious convictions which contradict the relevant concerns of a political society does not relieve the citizen from the discharge of political responsibilities."

This argument raises a question: what must be added to "mere possession" to create a valid claim against the state? When (if ever) does the Constitution require some individuals to be exempted from doing what society thinks is necessary to promote the common good? Conversely, what are the kinds of collective claims that rightly trump individual reservations?

Frankfurter offered a specific answer: social order and tranquility provide the basis for enjoying all civil rights—including rights of conscience and exercise. Indeed, all specific activities and advantages of government "presuppose the existence of an organized political society." Laws that impede religious exercise are valid when legislature deems them essential to secure civic order and tranquility. National unity is the basis of national security—a highest-order public value (as we would now say, a "compelling state interest"). National unity is secured, Frankfurter argued, by the "binding tie of cohesive sentiment," which is the "ultimate foundation of a free society." This sentiment, in turn, is fostered by "all those agencies of the mind and spirit which may serve to gather up the traditions of a people, transmit them from generation to generation, and thereby create that continuity of a treasured common life which constitutes a civilization."

If the cultivation of unifying sentiment is a valid end of government action, Frankfurter concluded, then courts should not interfere with legislative determinations of appropriate means. We do not know what works and what does not; we cannot say for sure that flag salutes are ineffective. In judging the legislature, we may use only the weakest of tests: is there any basis for the means the legislature has chosen to adopt? If there is, the courts must stay out.

But what if the state gets it wrong, goes too far, invades the fundamental rights and liberties of individuals or associations? Frankfurter answered this question, and concluded his opinion, with a profession of faith in the democratic process: it is better to use legislative processes to protect liberty and rectify error, rather than transferring the contest to the judicial arena. As long as the political liberties needed for effective political contestation are left unaffected, "education in the abandonment of foolish legislation is itself a training in liberty [and] serves to vindicate the self-confidence of a free people."

Justice (soon to be Chief Justice) Harlan Stone forcefully dissented. The law in dispute, he argued, did more than suppress and prohibit the free exercise of religion; it sought to coerce individuals to perform acts to which they are conscientiously opposed. Civil liberties, he argued, are "guarantees of freedom of the human mind and spirit and of reasonable freedom and opportunity to express them. . . . If these guarantees are to have any meaning they must, I think, be deemed to withhold from the state any authority to compel belief or the expression of it where that expression violates religious convictions, whatever may be the legislative view of the desirability of such compulsion."

Stone acknowledged that liberty guarantees are not absolute: the state has the right to do what it needs to do to "survive" and to protect basic interests, such as public order and health. These considerations suffice to justify measures such as the draft and mandatory vaccinations. But the very existence of protected civil liberties implies a restriction of government powers, an accommodation of public policy to the liberties in question. A valid end does not imply that all means in its pursuit are permitted. In the case of conflicts, whenever possible, there should be a "reasonable accommodation between them so as to preserve the essentials of both." Even if national unity is an important interest of the state, Stone argued, "there are other ways to teach loyalty and patriotism which are the sources of national unity, than by compelling the pupil to affirm that which he does not believe and by commanding a form of affirmance which violates his religious convictions."

There was no basis, Stone continued, for saying that the protection of civil rights should be left to legislatures; this was "no less than the surrender of the constitutional protection of the liberty of small minorities to the popular will." The Constitution is liberal as well as democratic. It "expresses more than the conviction of the people that democratic processes must be preserved at all costs. It is also an expression of faith and a command that freedom of mind and spirit must be preserved, which government must obey, if it is to adhere to that justice and moderation without which no free government can exist."

Despite his eloquence, Stone persuaded none of his brethren to follow him. Might he not be regarded as a noble but idiosyncratic voice? On the contrary: Frankfurter's opinion raised a storm of controversy the moment it was handed down, and many of the criticisms leveled against it at that time anticipated the kind of jurisprudence that emerged only a few years later and flowered in the following decades. Let me offer a few examples of these critiques, all published between 1940 and 1942.

William Fennell, a prominent member of the New York Bar, distinguished between the "liberal democrat" who "puts complete trust in the majority popular will to correct foolish legislation which violates . . . constitutional liberties" and the "liberal constitutionalist" who recognizes the important role of the Supreme Court in scrutinizing legislation that touches on the rights of minorities. The liberal democrat will use judicial review to safeguard individual rights—of speech, press, assembly, the franchise—needed to ensure the integrity of the democratic process. But only democratic majorities have the right to correct mistakes flowing from the exercise of procedural democracy. Arguing against Frankfurter's endorsement of the liberal democratic position, Fennell asked his readers to consider its consequences for previous decisions such as *Pierce*: wouldn't Frankfurter's jurisprudence have left every Catholic in the state of Oregon vulnerable to the anti-Catholic majority's repressive folly? He continued:

> If the "reconstructed court" (to use Frankfurter's own phrase in another case) continues to adhere in cases involving religious liberty to the doctrine of the majority in the *Gobitis* case, the scope of the state police power will be immeasurably enhanced and religious liberty will be at the mercy of shifting political majorities. It is to the lasting credit of the new Chief Justice [Stone] that he comprehended that the Constitution expresses more than the conviction that democratic processes must be preserved at all costs: it is also an expression of faith and a command which government itself must obey that freedom of mind and spirit must be preserved. This is the very "genius" of American constitutional democracy.

Writing in the *Michigan Law Review*, William F. Anderson noted that the *Gobitis* majority was of the opinion "that in questionable cases personal freedom could best be maintained by the democratic process as long as the remedial channels of that process functioned, . . . thereby distinguishing liberty of exercise of religion from liberty of speech, press, and assemblage in that the latter are indispensable to the remedial channels of the democratic process. . . ." Anderson worried that this process-based argument did not go far enough, either in theory or in practice: "If individual liberties are something more than the by-product of a democratic process, if in fact they have an intrinsic value worthy of protection, it is difficult to justify a decision which subordinates a fundamental liberty to a legislative program of questionable worth."

Reviewing the 1939–1940 term of the Supreme Court in the *American Political Science Review*, the redoubtable Robert E. Cushman declared that "all of the eloquence by which the majority extol the ceremony of flag saluting as a free expression of patriotism turns sour when used to describe the brutal compulsion which requires a sensitive and conscientious child to stultify himself in public."

What may well be regarded as the coup de grace was delivered by Thomas Reed Powell, Joseph Story Professor of Law at Harvard, a pioneering legal realist, and no softy. He was a liberal, but no one could accuse him of lacking spine. His article entitled "Conscience and the Constitution," published in a book entitled *Democracy and National Unity* (no merely theoretical topic in 1940) drips with scorn for the plaintiff Jehovah's Witnesses. Powell termed them "ignorant communicants of peculiar sects," "unreflecting, dogmatic, indoctrinated," "simple-minded and unintelligent." He even compared them to "mental defectives" and spoke approvingly of an education that weans the children away from the "nonsense of their parents."

And yet . . . Powell could not bring himself to accept Frankfurter's opinion. Three stumbling blocks proved insurmountable. First: as a matter of legal fact, he could not agree with Frankfurter's assertion that freedom of religion cannot be deployed against general legislation not specifically directed against religion. (The *Cantwell* decision, handed down a mere two weeks before *Gobitis*, had held just the reverse.) Second: as a practical matter, the effort to coerce children to salute the flag insincerely and contrary to conscience "seems . . . likely to be self-defeating" when measured against its goal of fostering patriotism and national unity. But finally, the case presented more than a question of practical policy. The issue of religious liberty was squarely on the table, in tension with the inculcation of national unity. By the logic of Frankfurter's own argument, if important constitutional values are in competition, then they must be weighed against one another. This the majority failed to do: "After general obeisance to religious freedom, almost no further weight is accorded to it in the opinion of the Court." In a serious weighing of competing values, Powell insisted, the Court must address quantitative as well as qualitative issues: how "important" is it to the nation to compel children to join in a patriotic ceremony which for them is idolatry? To what "extent" would exempting them impair the power of the state to preserve itself? Is the public interest "slight" or "major"? The Court must make a substantive choice, and that choice must rest on a judgment of relative significance. The majority's own language tacitly conceded this, citing the paramount importance of national unity; but Powell insisted that it failed to discharge its responsibility to assess what rests on the other side of the scale.

Judgments based more and less on clashing dimensions of value provide the basis for reasonable distinctions. If we decide that it is wrong to compel school children to salute the flag against conscience, does that mean that we must find in favor of conscientious objectors to military service? No, said

Powell: "No sensible person . . . can think it necessary. The differences of degree [in the state interests at stake] are too great." He continued:

> This is not to suggest that conscientious scruples can stand against all compulsion to do positive acts. Quite the contrary. The question is one of degree. I should think that it requires more justification to compel a man or child to commit what he regards as a sin than to restrict him in the areas in which he can practice what he regards as a command of the Lord. . . . The public need for coerced and insincere saluting of the flag by little children seems to me to be trivial . . .

The effects of these criticisms became apparent by 1942, when the Court decided the case of *Jones v. Opelika*. The facts were these: Jehovah's Witnesses had been going door-to-door selling religious books. Various municipalities enacted statutes requiring all booksellers to take out licenses and pay substantial fees in order to distribute books legally. The Jehovah's Witnesses refused to do so, citing free exercise claims as well as other arguments.

Writing for a five-man majority, Justice Reed began with the standard distinction between religious conscience and religious acts. He argued that, granting the presumption in favor of First Amendment freedoms, public determinations of time, place, and manner were rightly viewed as consistent with those freedoms. When proponents of religious views use "ordinary commercial methods" to propagate their view, fees and other regulations represent a "natural and proper exercise of the power of the State":

> Nothing more is asked from one group than from another which uses similar methods of propagation. We see nothing in the collection of a non-discriminatory licensing fee... from those selling books or papers, which abridges the freedoms of worship, speech, or press.

Led by Chief Justice Stone, four members of the Court dissented. In his opinion, Stone made two principal points. First, it is essential to examine the extent of the burden the law places on religious free exercise, which the majority blithely refused to do. The power to tax may well amount to the power to censor or suppress. Second, it does not suffice to say that the tax on speech and religion is "non-discriminatory." The First Amendment "is not confined to safeguarding freedom of speech and freedom of religion against discriminatory attempts to wipe them out. On the contrary, the Constitution, by virtue of the First and the Fourteenth Amendments, has put those freedoms in a preferred position."

Justice Murphy's dissent addressed Stone's questions and amplified his argument. The burden, Murphy insisted, was significant, and that fact was significant in resolving the case. To be sure, it was necessary to distinguish between burdens on thought and those on action. But this distinction should not be taken so far as to become unrealistic: "[E]ven an aggressive mind is of no missionary value unless there is freedom of action, freedom to communicate its message to others by speech and writing." Moreover, the defendants had failed to specify the harms to be avoided through the licensing system or to show that the statutes were drawn narrowly and precisely to address those evils. Nor, finally, would it do to argue that the statutes were for the purpose of raising general revenues rather than averting specific harms, because the "exercise, without commercial motives, of freedom of speech, freedom of the press, or freedom of worship are not proper sources of taxation for general revenue purposes."

> The mind rebels at the thought that a minister of any of the old established churches could be made to pay fees to the community before entering the pulpit. These taxes on petitioners' efforts to preach the "news of the Kingdom" should be struck down because they burden petitioners' right to worship the Deity in their own fashion and to spread the gospel as they understand it.

Even more significant than these two individual dissents was a brief dissenting statement jointly authored by three justices (Murphy, Black, and Douglas) who had formed part of the *Gobitis* majority. They wrote:

> The opinion of the Court sanctions a device which in our opinion suppresses or tends to suppress the free exercise of a religion practiced by a minority group. This is but another step in the direction which *Minersville School District v. Gobitis* took against the same religious minority and is a logical extension of the principles upon which that decision rested. Since we joined in the opinion in the *Gobitis* case, we think this is an appropriate decision to state that we now believe that it was also wrongly decided.

In the course of a comprehensive survey of the development of liberties protected under the Fourteenth Amendment, John Raeburn Green commented that while there was nothing good to be said about the majority decision, "[n]evertheless *Jones v. Opelika* . . . in the long run will mark an advance for [religious] liberty, because of the dissenting opinions." He was right, and sooner than he thought. In the very next year (1943), the replacement of Justice Byrnes, a member of the majority in *Opelika*, led to its reversal by a vote of 5 to 4 in the case of *Murdock v. Pennsylvania*. More remarkably, *Gobitis* was overruled by a stunning 6 to 3 vote, in *West Virginia v. Barnette*. I turn now to Justice Jackson's majority opinion, a highlight of which we have already encountered.

Jackson did not question that state's right to educate for patriotism and civic unity. But in his view, what was at stake was not education, rightly understood, but something quite different: "Here . . .we are dealing with a compulsion of students to declare a belief."

> [C]ensorship or suppression of expression of opinion is tolerated by our Constitution only when the expression presents a clear and present danger of action of a kind the State is empowered to prevent and punish. It would seem that involuntary affirmation could be commanded only on even more immediate and urgent grounds than silence. But here the power of compulsion is invoked without any allegation that remaining passive during a flag salute ritual creates a clear and present danger that would justify an effort even to muffle expression. To sustain the compulsory flag salute we are required to say that a Bill of Rights which guards the individual's right to speak his own mind, left it open to public authorities to compel him to utter what is not in his mind.

The issue, Jackson asserted, is not one of policy, that is, of effectiveness of means in pursuit of a legitimate end such as national unity. The prior question is whether the state possesses the rightful power to promote this end through compulsion contrary to conscience, a power the *Gobitis* majority assumed to inhere in our constitutional government. If it does not, then the issue is not exempting dissenters from otherwise valid policies, but rather reining in a state that is transgressing the bounds of legitimate action.

Jackson insisted that limited government is not weak government. Assuring individual rights strengthens government by bolstering support for it. In the long run, individual freedom of mind is more sustainable than is "officially disciplined uniformity." "To believe that patriotism will not flourish if patriotic ceremonies are voluntary and spontaneous instead of a compulsory routine is to make an unflattering estimate of the appeal of our institutions to free minds."

Limited government is not simply a wise policy, Jackson argued, it is also a matter of constitutional principle:

> The very purpose of a Bill of Rights was to withdraw certain subjects from the vicissitudes of political controversy, to place them beyond the reach of majorities and officials and to establish them as legal principles to be applied by the courts. One's right to life, liberty, and property, to free speech, a free press, freedom of worship and assembly, and other fundamental rights may not be submitted to vote; they depend on the outcome of no elections.

Limitations on government affect means as well as ends. There is no question that government officials and institutions may seek to promote national unity through persuasion and example. "The problem is whether under our Constitution compulsion as here employed is a permissible means for its achievement." It is in this context that Jackson penned his famous words about the fixed star in our constitutional constellation, the sphere of intellect and spirit that our laws protect from all official interference.

The three repentant justices who had issued promissory notes in their *Opelika* dissent redeemed them by joining the *Barnette* majority. Black and Douglas began their concurrence by noting that "since we originally joined with the Court in the *Gobitis* case, it is appropriate that we make a brief statement of reasons for our change of view." They offered three such reasons. First: as a constitutional matter, while the state can impose reasonable regulations on the time, place, or manner of religious activity, it can suppress religious liberty only to ward off "grave and pressingly immediate dangers." But the state was far from discharging its burden in this case; the danger was remote at best, and the policy only speculatively connected to its professed end. Second, the state's burden is especially heavy because the nature of the means employed—the statutory exaction of specific words—constitutes a form of "test oath" that has always been especially "abhorrent" in the United States. And even if this policy were constitutionally acceptable, it would be self-defeating: "Words uttered under coercion are proof of nothing but loyalty to self-interest. Love of country must spring from willing hearts and free minds, inspired by a fair administration of wise laws enacted by the people's elected representatives within the bounds of express constitutional prohibitions."

The third penitent, Justice Murphy, also concurred. Freedom of thought and religion, he contended, implies the right both to speak and to remain silent, except when compulsion is required for the preservation of an ordered society—as in the case of compulsion to testify in court. The compelled flag salute did not come close to meeting that test: its benefits were too indefinite and intangible to justify the restriction on freedom and invasion of privacy

Justice Frankfurter, the author of the majority opinion in *Gobitis*, penned a lengthy dissent, a personal apologia whose tone of injured dignity was set by its opening sentence: "One who belongs to the most vilified and persecuted minority in history is not likely to be insensible to the freedoms guaranteed by our Constitution." But he declared that what was at stake was not a constitutional question but rather a policy judgment. In this arena, courts should override legislatures only if reasonable legislators could not have chosen to employ the contested means in furtherance of legitimate ends. As a general proposition, there is a presumption in favor of legislatures, and legislation must be considered valid if there exists some rational basis for connecting it to a valid public purpose.

Exceptions to this presumption arise when the state employs constitutionally prohibited means. But the mandatory flag salute was not of this character. The state action at issue, Frankfurter asserted, was intended to promote or discourage religion, which was clearly forbidden. Rather, it was "a general non-discriminatory civil regulation [that] in fact [but not as a matter of intended effect] touches conscientious scruples or religious beliefs of an individual or a group." In such cases, it is the legislature's role to make accommodations, not the court's.

Jefferson and those who followed him wrote guarantees of religious freedom into our constitutions. Religious minorities as well as religious majorities were to be equal in the eyes of the political state. But Jefferson and the others also knew that minorities may disrupt society. It never would have occurred to them to write into the Constitution the subordination of the general civil authority of the state to sectarian scruples. The constitutional protection of religious freedom terminated disabilities; it did not create new privileges. It gave religious equality, not civil immunity. Its essence is freedom from conformity to religious dogma, not freedom from conformity to law because of religious dogma. The essence of the religious freedom guaranteed by our Constitution is this: no religion shall either receive the state's support or incur its hostility. Religion is outside the sphere of political government. This does not mean that all matters on which religious organizations or beliefs may pronounce are outside the sphere of government.

Many other laws (e.g., compulsory medical measures) have employed compulsion against religious scruples, but, said Frankfurter, courts have not struck them down:

> Law is concerned with external behavior and not with the inner life of man. It rests in large measure upon compulsion. . . The consent on which free government rests in the consent that comes from sharing in the process of making and unmaking laws. The state is not shut out from a domain because the individual conscience may deny the state's claim.

Indeed, Frankfurter asserted, it was wrong to describe the mandatory flag salute as compelled belief:

> Compelling belief implies denial of opportunity to combat it and to assert dissident views. Such compulsion is one thing. Quite another matter is submission to conformity of action while denying its wisdom or virtue with ample opportunity for seeking its change or abrogation.

In an oddly prophetic passage, Frankfurter contended that the majority's decision led to a reductio ad absurdum:

> Consider the controversial issue of compulsory Bible-reading in public schools. . . . Is this Court to . . . [deny] states the right to entertain such convictions in regard to their school systems, because of a belief that the King James

version is in fact a sectarian text to which parents of the Catholic and Jewish faiths and some Protestant persuasions may rightly object to having their children exposed? . . . Is it really a fair construction of such a fundamental concept as the right freely to exercise one's religion that a state cannot choose to require all children who attend public school to make the same gesture of allegiance to the symbol of our national life because it may offend the conscience of some children, but that it may compel all children [who] attend public school to listen to the King James version although it may offend the consciences of their parents?

Frankfurter concluded his dissent with a profession of political faith. Liberal democracy is more a matter of active, self-governing citizens than of protective or tutelary courts:

Of course patriotism cannot be enforced by the flag salute. But neither can the liberal spirit be enforced by judicial invalidation of illiberal legislation. . . . Only a persistent positive translation of the faith of a free society into the convictions and habits and actions of a community is the ultimate reliance against unabated temptations to fetter the human spirit.

CONCLUSION: JURISPRUDENCE AND THE MORAL BASIS OF LIBERAL DEMOCRACY

I have told this tale, not for its own sake, but with moral and political intent. I want to use these materials as a basis for testing our judgments about two questions. First: looking at the judicial bottom-line—the "holding"—are we more inclined to favor the outcome in *Gobitis* or in *Barnette*? Second: what kinds of broader principles underlie our judgment concerning these specific cases?

It is easy to sympathize with Frankfurter's dismay at the deployment of judicial review to immunize concentrated economic power against public scrutiny; with his belief that democratic majorities should enjoy wide latitude to pursue the common good as they see it; with his belief that the requirements of social order and unity may sometimes override the claims, however worthy, of individuals, parents, civil associations, and religious faith; and with his conviction that the systematic substitution of judicial review for democratic self-correction can end by weakening citizenship itself. Nonetheless, I believe (and I am far from alone), Frankfurter's reasoning in *Gobitis* was unsound, and his holding unacceptable. There are certain goods and liberties that enjoy a preferred position in our order and are supposed to be lifted above everyday policy debate. If religious liberty is a fundamental good, as Frankfurter acknowledges, then it follows that state action interfering with it bears a substantial burden of proof. A distant harm, loosely linked to the contested policy, is not enough to meet that burden. The harm must be a real threat; it must be causally linked to the policy in question; and the proposed remedy must do the least possible damage to the fundamental liberty, consistent with the abatement of the threat. The state's mandatory pledge of allegiance failed all three of these tests. *Gobitis* was wrongly decided; the ensuing public uproar was an indication that the Court had gone astray; and the quick reversal in *Barnette*, with fully half the justices in the new six-member majority switching sides, was a clear indication of the moral force of the objections.

We now reach my second question: is our judgment on these cases a particularized moral intuition, or does it reflect some broader principles? The latter, I think. What Justice Jackson termed the "sphere of intellect and spirit" is at or near the heart of what makes us human. The protection of that sphere against unwarranted intrusion represents the most fundamental of all human liberties. There is a strong presumption against state policies that prevent individuals from the free exercise of intellect and spirit. There is an even stronger presumption against compelling individuals to make affirmations contrary to their convictions. This does not mean that compulsory speech is always wrong; courts and legislatures may rightly compel unwilling witnesses to give testimony and may rightly punish any failure to do so that does not invoke a well-established principle of immunity, such as the bar against coerced self-incrimination. Even here, the point of the compulsion is to induce individuals to tell the truth as they see it, not to betray their innermost convictions in the name of a state-administered orthodoxy.

Gobitis and *Barnette* addressed the tension between public law and the religious conscience of Jehovah's Witnesses. But the majority decision in *Barnette* cast a wider net. While Justice Jackson's sphere of intellect and spirit includes religion, it encompasses much else besides. Does the expansion of protected liberty to include secular conscience make sense?

We may approach this question from two standpoints, the constitutional and the philosophical. Within constitutional law, both the narrow and expansive views have found proponents among able interpreters of the First Amendment. On the narrow side, Laurence Tribe argues that "The Framers . . . clearly envisioned religion as something special; they enacted that vision into law by guaranteeing the free exercise of religion but not, say, of philosophy or science." Christopher Eisgruber and Lawrence Sager object that "to single out one of the ways that persons come to understand what is important in life, and grant those who choose that way a license to disregard legal norms that the rest of us are obliged to obey, is to defeat rather than fulfill our commitment to toleration."

We see this debate playing out in a fascinating way in the evolution of the jurisprudence of conscience-based exemptions from the military draft. Section 6(j) of the WWII-era Universal Military Training and Service Act made exemptions available to those who were conscientiously opposed to military service by reason of "religious training and belief." The required religious conviction was defined as "an individual's belief in a relation to a Supreme being involving duties superior to those arising from any human relation, but [not including] essentially political, sociological, or philosophical views or a merely personal moral code."

In the case of *United States v. Seeger* (1965), however, the Court broadened the definition of religion by interpreting the statue to include a "sincere and meaningful belief which occupies in the life of its possessor a place parallel to that filled by the God of those admittedly qualifying for the exemption." Five years later, in *Welsh v. United States*, a Court plurality further broadened the reach of the statute to include explicitly secular beliefs that "play the role of a religion and function as a religion in life." Thus, draft exemptions could be extended to "those whose consciences, spurred by deeply held moral, ethical, or religious beliefs, would give them no rest or peace if they allowed themselves to become a part of an instrument."

It is not difficult to muster plausible constitutional arguments both supporting and opposing the expansion of religious claims to include secular conscience. But there are more general, extra-constitutional considerations that should incline us to favor a broader view. There are, I suggest, two features of religion that figure centrally in the debate about religiously-based exemptions from otherwise valid laws. First, believers understand the requirements of religious beliefs and actions as central rather than peripheral to their identity; and second, they experience these requirements as authoritative commands. So understood, religion is more than a mode of human flourishing. Regardless of whether an individual experiences religious requirements as promoting or rather thwarting self-development, their power is compelling. (In this connection, recall the number of Hebrew prophets — starting with Moses — who experienced the divine call to prophetic mission as destructive of their prior lives and identities.) My suggestion is that at least in modern times, some individuals and groups who are not religious come to embrace ensembles of belief and action that share these two features of religious experience — namely, identity-formation and compulsory power. If so, I would argue, it would make sense to expand the protections of religious liberty to cover these cases as well.

Like all politics, democratic politics is legitimate to the extent that it recognizes and observes the principled limits to the exercise of democratic power. The liberties that individuals and the associations they constitute should enjoy in all but the most desperate circumstances go well beyond the political rights that democratic politics requires. We cannot rightly assess the importance of politics without acknowledging the limits of politics. The claims that political institutions can make in the name of the common good coexist with claims of at least equal importance that individuals and civil associations make, based on particular visions of the good for themselves or for humankind.

Liberal democracy rightly understood must steer a principled course between theocratic claims that subject politics to a single religious orthodoxy and a civic republicanism that subordinates faith to the functional requirements of the polity. This means acknowledging that there are multiple sources of authority within a shared social space and that the relation among them is not straightforwardly hierarchical. As Chief Justice Hughes rightly observed in *Macintosh*, our conception of religious liberty implies that for some purposes, religious authority is higher than political authority and should take priority in cases of conflict between them.

This political pluralism may be messy and conflictual; it may lead to confrontations not conducive to maximizing public unity and order. Granted, it is essential to avoid anarchy. But the evidence linking accommodation of conscience to the bogey of political dissolution is scanty. And if political pluralism reflects the complex truth of the human condition, then the practice of politics must do its best to honor the principles that limit the scope of politics.

A key aim of liberal democratic politics is the creation of social space within which individuals and groups can freely pursue their distinctive visions of what gives meaning and worth to human existence. There is a presumption in favor of the free exercise of this kind of purposive activity (which I call "expressive liberty"), and a liberal democracy bears and must discharge a burden of proof whenever it seeks to restrict expressive liberty.

This standard for state action is demanding but not impossible to meet. While expressive liberty is a very important good, it is not the only good, and it is not unlimited. In the first place, the social space within which differing visions of the good are pursued must be organized and sustained through the exercise of public power; the rules constituting this space will inevitably limit in some respects the ability of individuals and groups to act as they see fit. Second, there are some core evils of the human condition that states have the right (indeed the duty) to prevent; to do this, they may rightly restrict the actions of individuals and groups. Third, the state cannot sustain a free social space if its very existence is jeopardized by internal or external threats, and within broad limits it may do what is necessary to defend itself against destruction, even if self-defense restricts valuable liberties of individuals and groups. A free society is not a suicide pact.

It may well be possible to add other categories of considerations that rebut the presumptions of conscience. In practice, the combined force of these considerations may warrant more restriction than accommodation. My point is only that the assertion of a conscience-based claim imposes a burden on the state to justify its proposed interference. There are many ways in which the state may discharge that burden, but if my position is correct, Justice Frankfurter's argument in *Gobitis* is not one of them. It is not enough to say that whenever a state pursues a general good within its legitimate purview, the resulting abridgement of conscience may represent unfortunate collateral damage but gives affected individuals and groups no legitimate grievance or cause of action. Claims of conscience are not trumps, but they matter far more than Frankfurter and his modern followers, such as Justice Scalia, are willing to admit.

Chapter Ten

Religion, Family, and Regime: The Case of Mormon Polygamy

The relation between religion and family policy cannot be explored in the abstract. I begin, therefore, by considering religion in America. It has four key characteristics that, taken together, render it unlike religion in any other country. American religion is socially pervasive, highly diverse, voluntary rather than ascriptive, and dynamically innovative. Each of these features has important implications for my topic. To mention only the last: religious innovation often generates new beliefs and practices that test established legal and cultural boundaries. This in turn raises questions about the limits of permissible pluralism.

The impact of American religion on family policy reflects, not only our religious particularity, but also our distinctive constitutional structures and traditions. Arguments about the limits of pluralism may begin as social controversies, but they inevitably end as constitutional contestation. At stake are not only the boundaries between different branches and levels of government but also the meaning of the religion clauses of the First Amendment and of the other liberty guarantees in the U.S. Constitution.

My overall thesis may be briefly stated. Given the distinctive features of U.S. religion and constitutionalism, there is a right way and a wrong way for American religion to contribute to public policy, concerning the family and more generally. The right way occurs when each faith tradition is regarded as a tributary nourishing the vast and heterogeneous expanse of American public culture, the body of understandings, norms, and aspirations from which we draw the premises of public dialogue. The wrong way occurs when a specific faith tradition asserts a comprehensive and unchallengeable dominion over all others, such that its premises and commitments enjoy dialogic primacy and are endowed with the force of law.

To investigate this thesis, I have selected a case study: the struggle, which occupied much of the nineteenth century, waged between the government of the United States and the Mormons over the issue of polygamy. Of great interest in its own right, this historical episode also helps illuminate some contemporary challenges to established understandings of marriage and family life.

BACKGROUND: A BRIEF HISTORY[1]

The Mormon Church was founded in 1830, the year of the publication of its new scripture, the Book of Mormon. Its founder and prophet, Joseph Smith, announced a separate revelation concerning plural marriage to his followers in 1843.

The issue of polygamy became public, and politically controversial, in the early 1850s. The platform of the first national convention of the Republican Party (1856) called for the abolition of both slavery and polygamy, which it linked under the rubric of the "twin relics of barbarism."

It did not take long for this new movement to work its way into public law. In 1862, a young congressman from Vermont, Justin Morrill, best known as the architect of the land-grant college system, successfully sponsored an "Act for the Suppression of Polygamy," which outlawed the practice throughout the U.S. territories. The Mormons resisted this law, and the federal government did not seriously try to enforce it during the Civil War and for some years thereafter.

As polygamy persisted, however, congressional impatience grew. Additional legislation passed in 1874 expanded the jurisdiction of federal courts over territorial affairs, setting the stage for a series of Supreme Court decisions that ultimately forced the Mormons to repudiate polygamy by the early 1890s.

Four cases proved critical. The first and best-known, *Reynolds v. United States* (1878), affirmed the constitutionality of congressional efforts to forbid the practice of polygamy in the U.S. territories.[2] In *Murphy v. Ramsey* (1885), the Court decided that Congress had the power to enact a law depriving polygamists residing in a territory of the right to vote.[3] *Davis v. Beason* (1890) expanded this power, holding that excluding from the franchise, not only practicing polygamists, but all members of the Mormon Church, was consistent with the religious free exercise clause of the First Amendment.[4] Later that year, the Court delivered the coup de grace in *The Late Corporation of the Church of Jesus Christ of the Latter-Day Saints v. United States*, holding that the Congress had the power to repeal the corporate charter of the Mormon Church and expropriate its assets.[5]

THE KEY CASES: A TEXTUAL ANALYSIS

It is not the purpose of this essay to explore in detail the legal issues raised by these cases. Rather, I want to highlight four themes that recur in the decisions and that illustrate what I regard as the wrong way to bring religion to bear on public policy.

Theme 1: The fight against polygamy represents a confrontation between civilization and barbarism.

In *Late Corporation*, for example, the Court declared that "the practice of polygamy [is] a crime against the laws, and abhorrent to the sentiments and feelings of the civilized world. . . . The organization of a community for the spread and practice of polygamy is . . . a return to barbarism."[6] In *Reynolds*, the Court linked the dichotomy between civilization and barbarism to geography and ethnicity: "Polygamy has always been odious among the northern and western nations of Europe, and, until the establishment of the Mormon Church, was almost exclusively a feature of the life of Asiatic and of African people."[7]

Theme 2: Polygamy is a direct violation of Christianity, which is made applicable to public policy through incorporation into the common law.

The incorporation of Christianity into the common law was one of the staples of nineteenth-century jurisprudence. Consider these representative statements from three of the most eminent U.S. students of the law prior to the Civil War. Joseph Story wrote that "one of the beautiful boasts of our municipal jurisprudence is that Christianity is part of the common law, from which it seeks the sanction of its rights, and by which it endeavors to regulate its doctrines." Thomas Cooley insisted that Christianity was part of common law jurisprudence "for certain purposes," primarily "those which relate to the family and social relations." For his part, James Kent declared that the common law's "direct and serious prohibition of polygamy [is] founded on the precepts of Christianity and the laws of our social nature, and . . . supported by the sense of practice of the civilized nations of Europe." Indeed, Chancellor Kent was willing to draw out and affirm the logical consequence — through the common law, Christianity enjoyed a unique, semi-established status in American society. As he declared in his famous decision in the *Ruggles* case (1811), common-law prohibitions against anti-Christian blasphemy do not extend to comparable statements about Islam "for this plain reason, that the case assumes that we are a Christian people, and the morality of this country is deeply engrafted upon Christianity, and not upon the doctrines or worship of these imposters." In vain did the aged Thomas Jefferson protest in

1824 that "the judges have usurped [legislative powers] in their repeated decision, that Christianity is part of the common law."[8]

Against this backdrop, it would have been remarkable if the Supreme Court had not appealed to Christianity in the Mormon cases. In *Davis*, the Court declared that "bigamy and polygamy are crimes by the laws of all civilized and Christian countries."[9] In *Late Corporation*, the Court insisted that "the principles of the law of charities [allowing the seizure of Mormon assets] are not confined to a particular people or nation, but prevail in all civilized countries pervaded by the spirit of Christianity."[10]

Theme 3: There is a strong rational basis for Christianity's antipathy to polygamy, because plural marriage is inconsistent with liberty and self-government.

Nineteenth-century courts regularly claimed that Christianity (and by that they meant Protestantism) was a necessary condition of political liberty. In 1824, for example, the Supreme Court of Pennsylvania declared that "no free government now exists in the world, unless where Christianity is acknowledged, and is the religion of the country." Twelve years later, the Supreme Court of Delaware added a historical gloss, remarking that "the tears and blood of revolutionary France during [the] reign of terror, when infidelity triumphed and the abrogation of the Christian faith was succeeded by the worship of the goddess of reason, [proved that] without [the Christian] religion no nation has ever yet continued free."[11]

The second step in this argument was the claim that Christianity's specific insistence on monogamy is essential to the broad foundation it provides for free government. In 1838, the eminent political theorist Francis Lieber argued that polygamy rests on the "patriarchal principle . . . which, when applied to large communities, fetters the people in stationary despotism, while that principle cannot exist long in monogamy."[12]

The Supreme Court incorporated these propositions into its decisions in the Mormon cases. In *Reynolds*, for example, the Court affirmed the linkage between the organization of marriage and the basic structure of political institutions: "According as monogamous or polygamous marriages are allowed, do we find the principles on which the government of the people, to a greater or lesser extent, rests."[13] The Court elaborated on this point seven years later in *Murphy*: "[N]o legislation can be supposed more wholesome and necessary in the founding of a free, self-governing commonwealth, fit to take rank as one of the coordinate States of the Union, than that which seeks to establish it on the basis of the idea of the family, as consisting in and springing from the union for life of one man and one woman in the holy estate of matrimony; the sure foundation of all that is stable and noble in our civilization; the best guaranty of that reverent morality which is the source of all beneficent progress in social and political improvement."[14] The Court did not explicitly invoke, but might well have cited, Article IV, Section 4 of the Constitution— "The United States shall guarantee to every State in this Union a Republican Form of Government"—for clearly the Court's position was that, without legal insistence on marriage as the union of one man and one woman, republican government itself was in jeopardy.

To say the least, this assertion stands in need of more scrutiny than it ever received in the Court's Mormon decisions. For example, the Mormon-dominated territorial legislature of Utah gave all women the right to vote in 1870, half a century before a similar guarantee became universal throughout the United States. The Female Suffrage Bill passed unanimously and without significant debate, an event, as historian Sarah Barringer Gordon observes, that was "unprecedented in the annals of woman suffrage."[15] Whatever the motives of the Utah legislature may have been, the incontrovertible fact remains that, with regard to one of the core rights of republican self-government, the Mormon community proceeded farther and faster than anyone else. Evidently the relation between family structure and political institutions is not as straightforward as the Court assumed.

Theme 4: The free exercise of religion is confined to the realm of inward faith and belief and does not extend to actions that express that faith and belief.

The canonical statement of this thesis occurs in the *Reynolds* decision. By the terms of the Free Exercise Clause, declared the Court, "Congress was deprived of all legislative power over mere opinion, but was left free to reach actions which were in violation of social duties or subversive of good order. . . . Laws are made for the government of actions, and while they cannot interfere with mere religious belief and opinions, they may with practices."[16]

At first glance, this distinction seems clear enough. But initial impressions are deceptive. Inherent in the logic of prohibiting religious conduct is the full apparatus of the criminal law, including criminal conspiracy, incitement, accessory after the fact, and so forth. In *Davis*, for example, the Court began by declaring that "few crimes are more pernicious [than are bigamy and polygamy] to the best interests of society and receive more general or more deserved punishment." The Court went on to reason that "if they are crimes, then to teach, advise and counsel their practice is to aid in their commission, and such teaching and counseling are themselves proper subjects of punishment, as aiding and abetting crime are in all other cases."[17] Through the machinery of the criminal law, in short, whenever religious belief is in fact linked to and inspires action, the constitutional distinction between belief and action is all but obliterated.

It is perfectly true that the bare claim of religious free exercise is not enough to immunize an act against legal scrutiny. As the Court said in *Late Corporation*, "the practice of suttee by the Hindu widows may have sprung from a supposed religious conviction. The offering of human sacrifices by our own ancestors in Britain was no doubt sanctioned by an equally conscientious impulse. But no one, on that account, would hesitate to brand these practices now, as crimes against society, and obnoxious to condemnation by the civil authority."[18] But the converse does not follow, that society has the right to criminalize whatever acts it chooses, regardless of the impact on religion. Because religious free exercise is a high constitutional value, public authority stands under an obligation to demonstrate a rational basis for laws that have the effect of burdening free exercise. It is not enough to say, as the Court did in *Late Corporation*, that the state has an unfettered right to prohibit polygamy as an "open offence . . . against the enlightened sentiment of mankind."[19] By that standard, all religiously inspired conduct is vulnerable to the shifting sands of public opinion.

In the Mormon cases, the Supreme Court was equally dismissive of the claim that religious belief can serve as the basis for a claim of exemption from legislation that pursues generally valid public purposes. As the Court ringingly declared in *Reynolds*, "as a law of the organization of society under the exclusive dominion of the United States, it is provided that plural marriages shall not be allowed. Can a man excuse his practices to the contrary because of his religious belief? To permit this would be to make the professed doctrines of religious belief superior to the law of the land, and in effect to permit every citizen to become a law unto himself. Government could exist only in name under such circumstances."[20]

This argument has a venerable pedigree, extending back at least to Hobbes's strictures against the exercise of private conscience. Nonetheless, constitutional jurisprudence throughout much of the twentieth century labored, with considerable success—in areas from employment to the military draft—to give weight to religious free exercise by creating a carefully delimited zone of accommodations and exemptions from otherwise binding legislation. History does not record that the Republic descended into anarchy.

CONCLUSION: LIVING HISTORY

It may seem that the debate over Mormon polygamy is of historical interest only. After all, post-nineteenth-century jurisprudence has completed the disestablishment of Christianity by disentangling religion and the common law. It is hard to imagine that a contemporary federal court would unabashedly argue from religious premises to policy conclusions. Indeed, a current-day Court faced with a new challenge to (or from) polygamists could not conceivably decide the case on the basis of the premises that motivated the nineteenth-century Supreme Court.[21]

In 1990, the Supreme Court swept away half a century of accommodationist jurisprudence and in effect reinstated *Reynolds* as the law of the land. This dramatic reversal reaffirmed a sharp distinction between religious belief and religiously inspired action and restored the identification of religion-based exemptions or accommodations with the evisceration of government itself—that is, with the principle of anarchy.[22]

This step raises a number of questions that citizens of the United States must ponder, as our population becomes ever more religiously diverse. Are we comfortable with the proposition that the bare fact of government's pursuit, through law, of generally valid public purposes is enough to nullify claims based on religious free exercise? Is the facial neutrality of the law enough to rebut objections, if there is evidence that the law is designed to target practitioners of a particular faith? When government does act in ways that burden religious free exercise, is it enough to cite offense to public opinion as justification, or must there be more robust links to concrete public concerns? Is it necessary and proper that, in a liberal democracy, the internal structure and practices of all subgroups (families, associations, faith communities) must mirror the constitutive principles of official public institutions?

The Mormon polygamy cases raise questions that bear on international as well as domestic questions. The principled opposition to polygamy forms an integral part of Christian theology, but not that of Islam.

This is not a trivial matter. While conflicts in the Middle East have focused attention on disputes over security and foreign policy, I would argue that disputes over sexual and family practices lie at the heart of the global encounter between the Islamic world and the West. Those whose outlook is formed by American culture criticize Islam for endorsing patriarchy. Those whose outlook is formed by Islamic beliefs criticize American practices for fostering licentiousness. To be sure, polygamy is controversial even within the Muslim world.[23] But while the carefully qualified contemporary Islamic defense of polygamy on grounds of social utility as well as Koranic authorization may fall strangely on Western ears, it calls for respectful dialogue rather than a priori rejection.[24] It would be sad if the lingering legacy of the repression of Mormon polygamy made such dialogue impossible.

The core issue in the polygamy cases—the relation between religion and free self-government—turns out to be remarkably contemporary. We are now in the early stages of a new great debate about the relation between culture and democracy. Those who argue that Islam is inherently incompatible with democracy often cite the persistence of patriarchy in the Muslim world as evidence. While I have offered some preliminary arguments in support of a looser relation between family structures and political regimes, I must acknowledge that this question remains open. It would be ironic indeed if the fallout from the "war on terror" provided retroactive vindication for some of the most religiously triumphalist statements in the history of U.S. jurisprudence.

NOTES

1. For these historical notes (and much more), I am indebted to Sarah Barringer Gordon, *The Mormon Question: Polygamy and Constitutional Conflict in Nineteenth Century America* (Chapel Hill: University of North Carolina Press, 2002).

2. 98 U.S. 145 (1878).

3. 114 U.S. 15 (1885).

4. 133 U.S. 33 (1890).

5. 136 U.S. 1 (1890).

6. 136 U.S. 1, at 48–49.

7. 98 U.S. 145, at 164.

8. For sources and further discussion, see Gordon, *The Mormon Question*, chap. 2.

9. 133 U.S. 333, at 341.

10. 136 U.S. 1, at 51.

11. Gordon, *The Mormon Question*, 73, 75.

12. *Ibid*, 81.

13. 98 U.S. 145, at 165–166. The Court went on to cite Lieber in support of this proposition.

14. 114 U.S. 15, at 57–58.

15. Gordon, *The Mormon Question*, 97.

16. 98 U.S. 145, at 164, 166.

17. 133 U.S. 33, at 341–342.

18. 136 U.S. 1, at 49–50.

19. 136 U.S. 1, at 50.

20. 98 U.S. 145, at 166–167.

21. This raises the obvious question of how a modern court *would* decide such cases. If polygamy went only one way, giving men opportunities denied to women, then the courts would probably strike it down as a violation of the Equal Protection Clause. But if the (hypothetical) law of polygamy treated men and women symmetrically, the question would become far more difficult. Precisely this issue is likely to arise if and when the first state officially legalizes gay marriage and the federal "Defense of Marriage Act" (110 Stat. 2419, 1996) is invoked against it. Because the Act defines marriage as a "legal union between one man and one woman," a challenge brought by gay couples would, if successful, open the door to a reconsideration of polygamy jurisprudence as well.

22. See *Employment Division v. Smith*, 494 U.S. 872 (1990).

23. While classical Islamic law grants the husband the right to have up to four wives simultaneously, many modern legal codes have curbed this right. Tunisia bans polygamy outright, and numerous Islamic nations have enacted legislation restricting this right, on various grounds. See John L. Esposito, *Women in Muslim Family Law*, 2nd ed. (Syracuse, NY: Syracuse University Press, 2001), 100–101.

24. Consider the following representative argument: "In times of war, populations become unbalanced due to the loss of men, leaving more women and orphans unprotected and without support. Therefore, it serves both a social and a moral function to include these surplus women, some of whom are perhaps widows with children, in a normal family unit." See Reem Sultan, "Marriage in Islam," zawaj.com/articles.

Chapter Eleven

Contending with Liberalism: Modern Catholic Social Thought (2004)

In his letter of invitation to this conference, Peter Steinfels formulated his charge to me in the following terms:

> While American Catholics have obviously worked out practical compromises with liberal pluralism, even in practice, and more so in theory, it is unclear whether Catholic social thought uses a moral vocabulary and indeed assumes a whole mindset alien to most Americans, including many Catholic Americans. . . . Catholic social teaching seems to offer a comprehensive idea of the good and put forth a vision of a harmonious social and political order. Liberalism eschews such comprehensive visions, is agnostic about the nature of the good, and accepts conflict and competition as more or less permanent, often productive features of society. . . . [We would like you to] assess where and to what extent the Catholic tradition tends to mesh or clash with the various conceptions of liberal pluralism—where you think there might be fruitful engagement—or where you think certain aspects of one tradition or the other are simply going to have to give way.

Let me begin by acknowledging what will soon become painfully apparent—my scanty knowledge of Catholic social thought, much of it acquired in a rush during the past few weeks (although I will admit to devouring the writings of John Ryan two decades ago). The topic is complicated by the fact that the terms *Catholic social thought* and *liberalism* each name a family of positions rather than a single stance, and these family differences become especially significant as proponents move from abstract philosophical principles to concrete public prescriptions.

In the nineteenth century, Catholic social thinkers ranged from outright reactionaries to genuine radicals, with shades of moderate and liberal reformers in between. Today, Catholic thinkers espouse diverse views on subjects such

141

as the merits of capitalist markets and the limits of state intervention. The editor of a recent collection of essays celebrating a century of Catholic social thought acknowledges that:

> The authors in this volume represent a decided tilt or bias toward Catholic progressivism, the Catholic left, and solidarity movements for justice in the church. We do not shirk from this choice. Others can celebrate the tradition in their own way.[1]

It is my impression that modern Catholic thinkers are sensitive to this distinction between principle and prescription, and to its implications for both thought and practice. Bryan Hehir asks,

> What authority should be attributed to teaching [i.e., legislative-policy advocacy] which is a mix of principles and policy choices? The [less activist, educational-cultural model of church activism] fears that this mix will mortgage the moral authority of the church. . . . The appropriate response is to distinguish levels of teaching and to espouse a procedural principle for teaching, that is, increasing empirical specificity means declining moral authority.[2]

More generally, a distinction is acknowledged between the church's universal moral principles, which bind in conscience, and its prudential policy choices, which require serious attention from Catholics but do not so bind.[3] Based on my readings, however, it appears that there is a great deal of unity on the plane of moral principle among Catholic social thinkers who disagree vehemently in their political and policy stances.

Matters are even more complicated within the family of liberal thinkers, who disagree both in practice and in principle. The practical differences over issues such as state intervention in the economy, the extent of permissible income redistribution, and the organization of educational systems are well known. Less well known, but equally significant for our purposes, are the increasingly intense theoretical debates among liberals over questions such as the following:

Is liberalism based (or can it be based) on a "comprehensive" religious, metaphysical, or moral doctrine, or must it be decoupled from such commitments?

If liberalism is seen as freestanding, are its principles known through intuition, or do they rest on an assumed consensus gentium which may be local rather than universal?

Is liberalism truly neutral with regard to substantive theories of the good, or does it necessarily presuppose some views of the good and rule out others?

Does liberal civic life accommodate, or rather rule out, public discourse and decisions based on comprehensive religious and metaphysical views?

Is there an authoritative liberal account of the human person, and, if so, does it offer an adequate account of moral motivation?

Can liberal society be theorized on the basis of individual self-interest, or is it necessary to introduce some moral principles that go beyond (and may contradict) self-interest?

May the liberal state intervene to promote a substantive vision of human development, or must it respect individual liberty except when its exercise jeopardizes the rights and interests of other individuals?

To what extent does the maintenance of liberal civic order and unity take priority over claims based on religious conscience, individual liberty, or the rights of parents?

Within the liberal tradition, each of these questions admits of a range of answers. The way in which a particular species of liberalism responds will determine the extent to which it is compatible with Catholic social thought. For example, forms of liberalism that in principle exclude religious discourse from the sphere of public deliberation are at odds with the basic public role of the modern Church. Similarly, it is impossible to reconcile Catholic social thought with the contention of "civic liberals" that in cases of conflict, the claims of individual conscience and religious free exercise must regularly yield to the requirements of citizenship and public order. But other variants of liberalism invoke substantive conceptions of the human good and see rights and duties, liberties and responsibilities, as intrinsically related and reciprocally limiting. The gap between these liberalisms and Catholic doctrine is far narrower.

Moreover, some of the classic Catholic critiques of liberalism rest on easily dispelled misunderstandings. For example, we learn from *Pacem in terris* that Catholic thought must reject any theory that grounds civic rights and duties, the binding force of the Constitution, or the government's legitimate authority, in the individual or collective will of human beings. But most liberal thinkers would likewise reject such theories. Anyone who believes, as did the authors of the Declaration of Independence, that individual rights are prior to government and that their protection is the central purpose of public life would resist grounding rights in human will.

Even those liberals who employ versions of social contract theory see consent as conferring legitimacy on governments and constitutions only when the circumstances of consent comport with moral requirements the force of which cannot be reduced to individual or collective will. For example, when the best-known contemporary liberal thinker, John Rawls, develops "justice as fairness," he insists that our choices lack public legitimizing force unless they occur within circumstances that reflect certain substantive moral views.

Finally, modern Catholic thought makes generous room for the principle of public consent. As Pope John XXIII states,

> It must not be concluded . . . because authority comes from God, that therefore men have no right to choose those who are to rule the state, to decide the form of government, and to determine both the way authority is to be exercised and its limits. It is thus clear that the doctrine which we have set forth can be fully consonant with any truly democratic regime. (*Pacem in terris*, 52)

I do not see how this teaching is fundamentally at odds with the underlying theory of liberal constitutionalism, that governments derive their just powers from the consent of the governed but that the permissible substance of that consent is delimited by the basic purpose of public institutions—the protection of individual rights and the promotion of the general welfare.

This convergence with liberal thought is strengthened by the manner in which modern Catholic doctrine coordinates individual rights and the common good:

> In our time the common good is chiefly guaranteed when personal rights and duties are maintained. The chief concern of civil authorities must therefore be to ensure that these rights are acknowledged, respected, coordinate with other rights, defended and promoted, so that in this way each one may more easily carry out his duties. (*Pacem in terris*, 60)

A final introductory remark concerns the ambiguity of the "liberal pluralism" with which Catholic social thought may stand in tension. At one level of analysis, this phrase can refer to a specific moral understanding, associated with the late Isaiah Berlin among others, according to which genuine goods and values are multiple, heterogeneous, mutually irreducible, non-hierarchically ordered, and (often) inharmonious. The wide range of choice-worthy and valuable human lives reflects the myriad ways in which human beings can choose among, combine, and balance these goods and values. For some liberals (and I count myself among them) this moral understanding offers the most persuasive justification for the basic tenets of liberal social philosophers. But other liberals disagree, either because they prefer some other foundation or because they reject the architectural metaphor entirely and view liberal social thought as freestanding.

It seems likely that Catholic social thought is incompatible with the philosophical account of moral/value pluralism, and therefore with any account of liberalism that takes philosophical pluralism as foundational. To the extent that Catholicism continues to embrace a natural law vision of the universe as cosmos or rational order, it seems committed to ultimate harmony among values and must reject any account of fundamental goods in conflict. And to the extent that Catholic morality takes its bearings from the imperatives of *imitatio dei*, it must subscribe to a theological version of a hierarchy of values, with Jesus' virtues at the apex.

At the other end of the spectrum is liberal pluralism understood in the manner of neo-Madisonian political science, as the division of society into conflicting and self-interested groups. Catholic social thought can certainly begin by acknowledging the fact of interest-group pluralism, but it cannot end there, for two reasons. First, Catholic social thought seems committed to the ideal of social harmony, and to the belief that the legitimate claims of each group can be brought together into a coherent and consistent whole. From this perspective, the clash of social interests is a sign that they have exceeded morally appropriate bounds. Second, Catholic social thought cannot remain satisfied with any account that reduces human motivation to self-interest. A sense of care for others and for the common good is within the moral powers of every human being and every citizen, and is therefore a basic demand of social morality. From this perspective, interest-group pluralism poses the problem, and Catholicism the solution.

There is a third sense of "liberal pluralism" with which Catholic social thought appears entirely compatible. I have in mind the theory, first developed by British thinkers such as Figgis, Barker, and Laski, that social life occurs in a number of associational venues, no one of which enjoys full authority over others. In particular, associations such as faith communities and families are not the creatures of political institutions and not wholly subject to their authority. This theory, which stands opposed to both Aristotelianism and French civic republicanism, leaves space for liberal freedoms of religious conscience and association as well as the distinction between public and private concernments. It is also compatible with Catholic teachings (as I understand them) concerning such matters as the independence of the Church and the authority of parents.

Finally, we reach the version of pluralism that seems most important for contemporary liberal theory and society—namely, deep and enduring differences among competing understandings of what gives meaning and purpose to human life. Many believe that liberalism as a social and political philosophy originated in the post-Reformation wars of religion. Viewed in this light, liberalism represented the effort to reconfigure the relationship between politics and religion such that a multiplicity of faiths could coexist within the same social space. This effort did not presuppose skepticism about religious truth-claims, let alone the relativist thesis that every faith tradition is equally true (or false). It flowed, rather, from the proposition that the human and moral costs of enforcing a single faith (even the True Faith) through coercive state power were prohibitive. More recently, liberal thought has generalized this argument for religious freedom and tolerance to include a wide (though not unlimited) range of differences among non-religious conceptions of the good life.

It goes without saying that liberal public orders cannot reasonably require Catholic social thought to relativize its theological and philosophical understanding of the human good. (Indeed, no individual or group can be required to do so, though some may try.) Nor, most liberals believe, must the bearers—individual or institutional—of Catholic social teachings confine their beliefs to the community of the faithful. The Church, leaders and laity alike, are free to bear witness in and to the larger society, and when necessary, articulate a critique of that society from the standpoint of "faithful citizenship." What liberalism requires, rather, is that the Church adopt a stance of severe and principled self-restraint in the face of the temptation to impose its beliefs on others through state coercion. As we will see, it is this requirement, the moral bedrock of liberal politics, that most squarely raises the specter of a clash between liberal principles and Catholic social thought.

SUMMARY OF A PROVISIONAL RESPONSE

With these considerations as backdrop, I can sketch my provisional response to Peter Steinfels's challenge as follows:

From the early stirrings of liberalism in the eighteenth century through the mid-twentieth century, the opposition between official institutional Catholicism and liberalism was stark. The clash between natural law-based organicist monism and individualistic pluralism was at the heart of this historic opposition. As David O'Brien puts it,

> The problem of *Quadregesimo Anno* . . . was that its proposed Christian social order would be difficult, perhaps impossible, to implement in a pluralistic society. How could differing interest groups be persuaded to subordinate group interests to the general welfare? More important, who would define the specific requirements of the common good? The church had always regarded the democratic answer of negotiation and compromise as incompatible with natural law. . . . Refusing to acknowledge the legitimacy of pluralism, [the popes prior to Vatican II] could hardly understand the necessarily messy, ambiguous ways of democratic politics.[4]

Since then, the gap between Catholicism and liberalism has narrowed significantly. Much of the movement has occurred on the Catholic side. For the purposes of this chapter, I will take it as given that mainstream Catholicism

has made its peace with constitutional democracy, rights of religious conscience, and individual liberties generally. Indeed, this reconciliation is now
expressed in the language of principle rather than of regrettable necessity or
modus vivendi. To quote O'Brien once more:

> [John XXIII's] list of human rights included both the social and economic rights
> developed in the social encyclicals and the political and civil rights, including
> the right to religious liberty, about which the popes had long seemed more
> doubtful. Because they drew heavily on neo-scholastic philosophical categories,
> John's encyclicals recalled those of Leo XIII, but now these affirmations of hu-
> man dignity and human rights were placed in a democratic context: individuals
> and states had the obligation to share responsibility for constructing institutions
> in which these rights could be protected. . . . With the changes of the Second Vat-
> ican Council, especially the Declaration on Religious Liberty, Catholics could
> explore the requirements of citizenship (as done, for example, by John Courtney
> Murray and, more recently, by the United States Bishops) without the inhibi-
> tions the older church even at its best had imposed.[5]

Two of the most important reconciliations with liberalism have come in the
areas of freedom of expression and religious pluralism. Regarding freedom of
expression, the *New Dictionary of Catholic Social Thought* observes that

> In *Pacem in terris* John XXIII abandoned the earlier papal emphasis on censor-
> ship and recognized a person's moral right to freedom in expressing and com-
> municating his feelings. Though a person may think and speak incorrectly, the
> pope insisted that a distinction be made between error and the person who errs.
> Thus, errors must be rejected, but people in error must be allowed to speak so
> that they might break through their mistakes and make available to everyone oc-
> casions for the discovery of truth.[6]

Even more significant is the shift in the sphere of religious pluralism,
which implies a fundamental shift in the relationship between the Church and
public authority. Hehir notes that:

> In the nineteenth century church-state controversies (Gregory XVI to Leo XIII),
> religious pluralism was an exception to be tolerated when it could not be over-
> come. . . . In the teaching of Vatican II religious pluralism was . . . the accepted
> setting in which the church pursued its ministry in freedom, dependent only on
> its own resources and the quality of its witness.[7]

In our time, accordingly, the freedom of the Church is understood as requiring not a favored, publicly authorized position in society but only the protected ability to be socially engaged.[8] This new understanding of the role of
the Church in a pluralistic society is laid out most lucidly in *Gaudium et spes*.

In that document, it is argued that there is a clear distinction between the Church and the political community. The Church's core activities rest on the power of God rather than of the civil authorities. While the Church makes use of "things of time," it is a sign and safeguard of the transcendence of the human person. While the political community and the Church are mutually independent and self-governing, each works in its own way for the good of the person. The service of both church and state works better if there is mutual cooperation. At the least, earthly powers must not impede the liberty of the Church to carry out its distinctive mission—to preach the faith, teach the social doctrine, discharge its human duties, and pass moral judgment on politics as well as social questions when necessary.[9]

Despite these manifold engagements with pluralism, some continue to wonder whether modern Catholic doctrine is yet adequate to the new social reality that it is encountering. John Colemen puts it this way: "Catholic social thought too easily assumes the possibility of social harmony. . . . [It] has not really faced the full reality of pluralism, especially the political implications of living in societies with especially deeply diverging views on fundamental social values.[10]

At first glance, this suggestion is perplexing, at least to an outsider. As we have already seen, the modern Church has abandoned all theocratic claims, acknowledged a separation between church and state authority, recognized the fact of religious pluralism, and endorsed the principles of freedom of expression and freedom of conscience. This would seem to be enough to allow the Church to coexist stably with modern societies containing deep differences on social values. (Of course, the Church claims the authority to declare a unity of fundamental principles binding on the conscience of all its members, but that is not directly a question bearing on public order.)

Nonetheless, there do seem to be enduring tendencies that tug against the principled opening to modern social pluralism. As Hehir points out, in contradistinction to liberal political philosophy, "Catholic teaching holds that society and the state are organic developments rooted in the nature of the person. This premise inclines Catholic teaching to accord a broad role to the state, particularly in pursuit of moral and religious values."[11]

It is not hard to see how this self-confident organicism might spill over into stances that non-Catholics (or even Catholic dissenters) could rightly view as the oppressive use of state power. At the highest religious or metaphysical level, the lingering influence of Thomism may bolster this organicism by leading Catholic thought to give too much weight to the idea of universal rational order at the expense of divine grace and inscrutability as supervening on rational knowledge, and of human sinfulness as a disruption of God's order.

Even if the concept of a singular divine order is maintained, pluralism enters through the range of possible interpretations of that concept—differing theological orientations that develop around a range of theological metaphors. In the Catholic tradition, God has been variously understood as the good shepherd, as the intelligent designer, as an historical journeyer with humanity, or as social liberator. Each of these images finds warrant in canonical texts and human experience; each leads to a distinctive understanding of the person, society, and social action. One may wonder whether the Church fully acknowledges the force of this internal pluralization, which can lead to a wide range of practical stances and prescriptions.

Even if one denies the force of these pluralizing tendencies in the name of an ensemble of knowable and authoritative social truths, individuals and groups are likely to stand in differing relations to those truths. Even if the public order has the right to encourage knowledge of social truth, it does not always, or usually, have the right to repress falsehood. (That is presumably the point of Pope John XXIII's distinction between error and the person who errs.)

There is, however, another crucial distinction, between maintaining error and acting on error. As I understand it, the Church believes that it is not wrong for the state to repress the erroneous action, even when the nature or fact of the error is socially disputed—that is, even when the Church's moral position is not universally accepted. To take a familiar example: while the members of a political community may agree that all persons are entitled to certain enforceable protections, they may disagree about the nature of personhood. The Church teaches that fetuses are persons; others have different views. If the Church were able to persuade a solid majority of American citizens of its position, it might be able to reverse the nation's current constitutional-legal stance and use the power of the state to outlaw abortion. Presumably the Church would feel no qualms about so acting. But those who take their bearings from the fact of deep moral disagreements in society might well have a principled hesitation about taking this step.

On the other hand, sophisticated contemporary liberal theorists (John Rawls is the leading example) distinguish between "reasonable" and "unreasonable" pluralism. State authority may not deploy its coercive power against reasonable positions, because it is possible for the proponents of all such positions to reach rational agreement on the fundamental principles of social order; not so for the unreasonable. Within its own teaching, it would seem that the Church has the right to make the same distinction and to act accordingly. The debate would then turn to competing conceptions of the morally reasonable. One may doubt that there is a neutral position from which to conduct this debate.

CATHOLIC SOCIAL THOUGHT AND LIBERAL THEORY

It may prove useful, in conclusion, to conduct a more systematic comparison between the basic tenets of Catholic social thought and those of liberal theory. As a point of reference, I will use the nine-point account of Catholic social teachings in the *Encyclopedia of Catholicism*. This section will set forth each point and offer a commentary from a liberal-theoretical perspective.

Point 1: "The foundational concept of the social teachings is the sacredness or dignity of the human person."
    Commentary: Many contemporary liberals take human dignity as their point of departure. Some ground that dignity theologically (human beings made in God's image). Others proceed in a Kantian manner: our dignity is rooted in our liberty, which is a "fact of reason." Still others ground human dignity in moral intuition, or in a consensus gentium.
    The liberal account of dignity diverges from Catholicism in a number of key respects. First, while liberal dignity is compatible with a divine foundation, it does not require it. Second, liberals are inclined to interpret dignity as moral freedom, with few restraints placed on the use of that freedom other than respecting the like freedom of all other individuals. For example, many liberals contend that under suitable circumstances, suicide is consistent with respect for human dignity. Third, liberalism embraces a range of views on the nature of human personhood, some of which include, while others exclude, beings whom Catholics place in the category of persons.

Point 2: "Catholic social teachings draw a direct line from human dignity to human rights and duties. Human rights are moral claims to goods of the spiritual and material order that are necessary to protect and promote human dignity. Duties are responsibilities that flow from the person's status as a creature (duties toward God) and from the social bonds one has in the human community (duties toward others)."
    Commentary: Many liberals would accept the Catholic account of rights as encompassing affirmative claims as well as negative protections. It is not clear on its face precisely which spiritual and material goods are required to promote human dignity, but liberals need not disagree with Catholic social thought on the particulars, many of which (e.g., those enumerated in *Pacem in terris* 11-27) liberal thinkers would regard as both familiar and acceptable. Moreover, liberals agree that rights and duties are correlative, that it is logically impossible to claim a right without simultaneously asserting others' duty to respect that right. While all liberals acknowledge social duties, some deny that the person must be understood as a creature and therefore do not acknowledge duties toward God.

Point 3: "A central dimension of Catholic social philosophy is its stress on the social nature of the person. Society and state are natural extensions of the social nature of the person."

Commentary: Liberals need not, and most do not, deny the social dimension of personhood. No one can reasonably doubt that normal human development requires social bonds, or that many important human goods can only be realized in and through society. At the same time, there is an important ambiguity in the idea of state and society as natural extensions of the person. Society is—as Aristotle himself suggested—a combination of natural inclination (or need) and human artifice (or choice). Not all social and political forms are equally hospitable to the development of the human person. From a teleological standpoint, some forms are more "natural" than others are.

Point 4: "The state-society distinction is a complement to the distinction of the common good and public order. The common good . . . is the complex of spiritual, temporal, and material conditions needed in society if each person is to have the opportunity to develop his or her human potential. . . . The public order is that part of the common good that properly belongs to the state. It is constituted by the goods of public peace, public morality, and the enforcement of basic standards of justice. . . . The effect of distinguishing the terms common good and public order is to limit the role of the state."

Commentary: Liberals are often thought to deny the existence of the common good. And this is true, to the extent that the common good is understood as distinct from and even opposing the good of individuals. Notably, the Catholic view does not do this. Catholic social thought defines the common good as the social space within which each individual can realize his or her own good. It is a complex empirical-sociological question whether such a social space is possible— that is, whether the conditions for the development of each individual can be harmonized in practice with the conditions of all others. (Catholics may well be more inclined to assume the possibility of harmony than are most liberals.)

Moreover, liberal theory is entirely comfortable with the state/society distinction and with the thesis that important human goods are found within voluntary associations independent of the state. Far from being alien to liberal theory, the assertion of inherent limits to the legitimate role of the state is widely regarded as one of liberalism's defining features. (The location of the boundary between state and society, or between the public and the voluntary, has always been contested and remains so today.)

Point 5: "The state-society relationship is evaluated in Catholic thought by the principle of subsidiarity and the concept of socialization. Subsidiarity . . . seeks to preserve as much freedom in society as possible, by contending that responsibility for addressing social questions should begin with the local or smallest institutional authority and be referred to the state only when it becomes clear that other institutions cannot fulfill the need. . . . The state has positive moral responsibilities and is the ultimate guarantor of the rights of the person in society. . . . Socialization is the product of increasing complexity in society, generated by the growing involvement of the state in the socioeconomic order. [Pope John XXIII] saw this enhanced role of the state as a method of satisfying human rights."

Commentary: This point marks a difference, at least of emphasis, between Catholic and liberal thought. Not all liberals accept the principle of subsidiarity; some believe that to promote a wide range of overarching public purposes, the central state is justified in overriding the authority of families, voluntary associations, and local public authorities. Not all believe that the maximization of social freedom is the single dominant value that should determine social organization. Nor do all liberals accept the concept of socialization; some argue, conversely, that increases in economic and social complexity have outrun the ability of state mechanisms to govern these processes knowledgeably and efficiently. For them, the logical implication of complexity is the reduction of the state's role in favor of markets and voluntary associations.

Point 6: "In the social space beyond the control of the state in society, Catholic teaching locates the role of intermediate associations, often called voluntary associations in Western society. These groups come together by the choice of citizens; while not under the auspices or control of the state, they exist for public purposes."

Commentary: Since at least de Tocqueville's time, intermediate associations ("civil society") have been a leitmotif of liberal social thought. After a period of eclipse in the mid-twentieth century, neo-Tocquevilleanism surged and now stands at the center of liberal social inquiry.

The extent to which intermediate associations are beyond the control of the state is contested, however. Some liberals are more inclined to empower the state to enforce general public norms within such associations, with controversial consequences. For example, some public authorities have demanded the right to enforce principles of non-discrimination against associations that exclude women, while others would deny organizations such as the Boy Scouts the right to exclude individuals on the basis of sexual orientation. The legal and constitutional resolution of these disputes frequently revolves around the question of whether particular associations should be regarded as carrying out public purposes in a manner that bring them within the purview of legitimate state regulation.

Point 7: "Permeating the entire structure of Catholic social teachings is their theory of justice. . . . The theory of justice distinguishes commutative, distributive, and social justice, with the latter category providing the dominant framework for the social teaching."

Commentary: Modern liberalism focuses on theories of justice as well, with a noticeable shift from commutative to distributive questions in recent decades. If it is correct to understand social justice as the fair and equal opportunity to participate in public institutions and social processes that promote a good society, then liberalism embraces social justice as well.

Point 8: "John Paul II uses the concept of solidarity as a central theme in his social teaching. . . . [He] sees solidarity as analogous to charity; it assumes in his teaching the status of virtue. The principal role solidarity has is to direct the dynamic of interdependence, which is reshaping the socioeconomic life and societies and the international community. In a world of increasing interdependence, a vision of solidarity is needed as the foundation for just relationships."

Commentary: There is a direct analogue in liberal thought to the concept of solidarity, namely, the characteristic liberal tendency toward moral universality that transcends particular attachments and identities. From this universalistic standpoint, it is unreasonable and wrong not to care about the suffering of some fellow human beings, just because they happen not to be members of one's family, tribe, ethnic group, or political community. Liberals disagree among themselves concerning the morally acceptable balance between particular attachments and universal concerns. But all are inclined to attach moral weight to the idea of a common humanity. It was liberals, after all, who took the lead in developing a conception of universal human rights, of the right and duty of the world community to enforce these rights against sovereign states that systematically violate them.

CONCLUSION

If the analysis presented in this chapter is even roughly accurate, then one must conclude that the gap between Catholic social thought and liberal theory is much narrower than it was in the mid-nineteenth century, or even in the mid-twentieth. On the one hand, Catholicism has made its peace with constitutional democracy, individual rights, freedom of religious conscience, and the separation of church and state. On the other hand, liberals are less inclined than they once were to emphasize self-interest at the expense of moral motivation, negative liberty at the expense of social justice, or rights to the exclusion of natural duties. Liberals are happy to reject "atomism" in favor of the social embeddedness of individuals—that is, as long as the social nature of personhood is not employed to deprive individuals of personal and political liberties.

Important differences remain, however. Some liberals embrace skepticism or relativism about the human good; some downplay the moral role of the state or seek to exclude faith-based arguments from public discourse; some emphasize the civic prerogatives of the state at the expense of family and associational autonomy. Clearly Catholics must reject these versions of liberalism. Liberals for their part must resist the Catholic use of controversial theses in theology and natural law as the basis of coercive state policy. It is one thing for Catholics reasoning within the premises of their community to reach conclusions about abortion, assisted suicide, and homosexuality that are held to be binding on the faithful; quite another to impose those views on others. Catholics may be affronted by a legal code that permits acts they view as abominable. But in circumstances of deep moral diversity, the alternatives to enduring these affronts may be even worse.

NOTES

1. John A. Coleman, "Introduction: A Tradition Celebrated, Reevaluated, and Applied." in Coleman, ed., *One Hundred Years of Catholic Social Thought* (Maryknoll, NY: Orbis Books, 1991), 5.

2. J. Bryan Hehir, "The Right and Competence of the Church in the American Case," in Coleman, *One Hundred Years*, 68.

3. "Modern Catholic Social Thought," in Judith A. Dwyer, ed., *The New Dictionary of Catholic Social Thought*, 614.

4. David O'Brien, "A Century of Catholic Social Teaching," in Coleman, *One Hundred Years*, 19-20.

5. *Ibid*, 22-24.

6. Dwyer, *The Dictionary of Catholic Social Thought*, 623.

7. Hehir, "The Right and Competence," 63.

8. *Ibid*, 59-61.

9. Summary of *Gaudium et spes*, 76.

10. Coleman, "Neither Liberal nor Socialist: The Originality of Catholic Social Teaching," in Coleman, *One Hundred Years*, 39.

11. Hehir, "The Right and Competence," 64.

Chapter Twelve

Traditional Judaism and American Citizenship

From the destruction of the Second Temple to the onset of modernity, few Jewish communities held the status of full citizenship in the jurisdictions in which they dwelled. Many communities enjoyed a measure of administrative autonomy, but their relationship to the larger polity was fragile. Rights and powers extended to Jews were contingent on the good will and self-interest of the sovereign and were often reduced or revoked as circumstances changed. For the most part, Jewish politics consisted in a kind of diplomacy with authorities who were in effect external powers.

With the rise of the modern nation-state, two other possibilities emerged. Some nations offered Jews citizenship on the condition that they abandon Judaism, at least as traditionally understood and practiced. A smaller number—the United States among them—were prepared to accept Jews as citizens without such onerous conditions. Article VI of the U.S. Constitution declared that "no religious test shall ever be required as a qualification to any office or public trust under the United States." (By contrast, it was not until 1858 that Jews were permitted to occupy seats in the British House of Commons![1]) Three years after the ratification of the Constitution, the adoption of the First Amendment guaranteed the free exercise of religion for all faiths. From the earliest years of the Republic, Jews eagerly embraced this generous offer of equality with dignity.

Citizenship is not an unmixed blessing, however. It implies burdens as well as benefits, and it may impose requirements on citizens that challenge the requirements of their faith. U.S. citizenship poses some distinctive challenges for Jews. Consider the following: both Judaism and the United States rest on a fundamental and supremely authoritative text, made binding at a specific historical moment. Both see the text as constituting the core identity of their

155

respective peoples. Both understand the authority of the text in covenantal terms. To apply that text to particular problems, both have developed elaborate traditions of interpretation, which have taken on a standing virtually equal to the text itself. And each text yields judgments and laws that are taken to be binding. On its face, this relationship would seem fraught with opportunities for conflict.

There are complications, however. The nature of the relationship between American Jews and the American polity depends crucially how they understand their relationship to Judaism and to the United States. Some Orthodox Jews view their status in the United States as parallel to that of their ancestors in Poland: they are sojourners in a land not their own, prepared to take advantage of whatever opportunities may arise to widen the space for the unfettered practice of their faith. This may well involve the artful use of ballot-box strength as a negotiating tool, but the relationship of these Jews with the American polity is largely instrumental. A life obedient to Torah is the end; political arrangements are at best means in service of that end. A relationship between Judaism and America understood in this fashion produces some practical difficulties, but no deep issues of principle.

At the other end of the spectrum are those American Jews who view the Torah and halachic law as matters of cultural and historical significance but not as sources of authority on a par with secular law. For them, the guarantee of religious free exercise confined to private life is sufficient. Indeed, they may well be most comfortable with an arrangement in which all faiths in the American polity agree to regard the private sphere as their appropriate realm. Here, as in the case of the Orthodox, some practical difficulties may arise, but not conflicts touching on fundamental principles.

The most interesting and complex problems arise in the case of Jews who simultaneously define themselves as "traditional"—that is, who understand Judaism in classically religious terms—*and* regard themselves as conscientious U.S. citizens rather than sojourners. Although I would not characterize myself as a traditional Jew, strictly speaking, I will focus on this group as the basis for exploring some aspects of the relationship between Jews and the American polity.

I take the heart of Jewish traditionalism to be the commitment to certain texts as authoritative, to the interpretation of these texts as a necessary condition for prudent and moral action, and to the community and tradition of interpreters as the touchstone for reflection on practical issues here and now. Accordingly, my remarks will revolve around a handful of key Biblical and Talmudic texts that for millennia have served as touchstones in debates over the proper Jewish stance toward politics. And because I am a political theorist by training, I will deploy these texts to address some of the classic questions of political theory as well. While this procedure does not yield concrete answers to specific political problems, it can at least help us to orient ourselves.

It is of the essence of a tradition that develops in community over time that it contains within itself a range of defensible but competing interpretations. Both Judaism and U.S. constitutional jurisprudence manifest this internal plurality. I would suggest that there are interpretations of traditional Judaism that are more and less hospitable to the conscientious practice of U.S. citizenship, and likewise interpretations of American constitutionalism that are more and less hospitable to the practice of traditional Judaism. It is appropriate, I believe, for traditionalist American Jews to seek out the legitimate possibilities of each tradition that will minimize the tension between them.

THE NATURE OF POLITICAL LIFE

From the onset of modernity, many Jews have been attracted to romantic/ optimist political creeds, at the heart of which is the assumption that human beings are fundamentally good (or at least perfectible) and that suffering and evil result from the oppressive and unjust ordering of institutions. Traditional Jews cannot accept this assumption. Immediately after God vows to Noah never again to unleash destruction on the human race as a whole, we read, "The impulse of man's heart is evil from his youth" (Genesis 8:21). Evil is permanent because it is rooted in our nature.

Jews do not take this fact to imply that our impulses are *only* evil, or that our sin is so deep-rooted, so "original" that we are powerless against it. Nor does it mean that human institutions are powerless in the face of our evil inclinations. But it does suggest that the structure of those institutions, and our understanding of them, must reflect the ineradicableness of evil. In one of the most familiar sections of the Talmud, *Pirkei Avot*, we find the following statement: "Were it not for fear of the political ruler men would swallow one another alive" (Mishnah Avot 3:2). Indeed, the first duty of public authorities is to prevent this from happening, by securing the peace and public order. Not only are these goods in themselves; they are the conditions for the effective pursuit of higher-order goods, public or communal; all the more for communities (such as American Jews) that constitute small minorities within the polity.

From this standpoint, it should not be difficult for traditional Jews to acknowledge the importance of the "domestic tranquility" cited in the Preamble to the Constitution as one of the core purposes of our institutions. Nor should they stumble at the threshold of Madisonian realism as the basis of those institutions; there is nothing in the strategy of counterposing interest to interest, passion to passion, ambition to ambition that contradicts the moral understanding of traditional Judaism. Impartial judges and public-spirited executives are always to be sought, and prized as treasures when we find them. But because we cannot count on individual goodness and virtue of citizens or leaders, we must arrange our institutions with an eye to avoiding the greatest evils, even when those who decide and act within them are less than wholly good.

CLAIMS OF POLITICS AND CLAIMS OF FAITH

One might imagine that traditional Judaism would tend toward theocracy. One can certainly find examples of theocracy in the Bible. During the founding of the modern state of Israel, there were many traditionalists who urged the supremacy of religious over political authorities and who were bitterly disappointed when this failed to develop. Isaac Halevi Herzog, a prominent rabbinic authority who welcomed the establishment of the state, writes that he "aspired to create a powerful movement among us whose purpose would be to influence the future legislative council to include in the constitution a basic clause stipulating that the law of the state will be Torah law."[2] For him, it was "inconceivable that the laws of the Torah should allow for two parallel authorities."[3]

If traditional Judaism were unequivocally theocratic, this would create a deep gulf between Judaism and American constitutional politics, which is emphatically anti-theocratic. Fortunately for traditionalist American Jews, there is a long line of Biblical and Talmudic interpretation that leads to at least a qualified endorsement of secular government.

The discussion takes as its point of departure the establishment of kingship. Gideon famously refused the people's demand that he become king over Israel: "I will not rule over you myself; nor shall my son rule over you; the Lord alone shall rule over you" (Judges 8:23). There was a problem, however; the Lord ruled, not directly, but through human intermediaries. What would happen when these theocratic authorities, the "judges," strayed from the true path? Samuel, the last of the judges, was a righteous man, but his sons were not: "they were bent on gain, they accepted bribes, and they subverted justice." The leaders of the people gathered to request that Samuel "appoint a king for us, to govern us like all the other nations." Samuel resisted their demands, to no avail. The elders insisted that the administration of justice and the conduct of war made kingship necessary: "We must have a king over us . . . [to] rule over us and go out at our head and fight our battles." In the end, the Lord said to Samuel, "Heed their demands and appoint a king for them" (1 Samuel 8).

Although the Lord also tells Samuel that the people's demand for a king means that "it is Me they have rejected as their king," the Bible does not characterize kingship as wrong in the same way that idolatry is wrong. Indeed, the period before kings is linked to stories of strife and disorder. Without a king, "everyone did as he pleased." It seems that the establishment of non-theocratic authority was needed to prevent the Jewish people from swallowing one another alive. Rightly understand, kings can perform limited but critical non-theological functions: ensuring public order, administering justice, and safeguarding the people against external danger.

As the discussion of this matter developed during the Talmudic and medieval periods, kingship became a metaphor for secular government in general, not a particular form of political regime. Nissim Gerondi, a leader of the Barcelona Jewish community, argued explicitly for two "separate agencies," one to judge the people in accordance with Torah law, the other to uphold public order. The precedent for this, he insisted, was established during the Biblical period: "at a time when Israel had both Sanhedrin and king, the Sanhedrin's role was to judge the people according to just [Torah] law only and not to order their affairs in any way beyond this, unless the king delegated his powers to them." Gerondi accepted that the secular authority would need to use coercion "to enhance political order and in accordance with the needs of the hour," even if the application of force is "undeserved according to truly just [Torah] law." He went so far as to acknowledge that "some of the laws and procedures of the [gentile] nations may be more effective in enhancing political order than some of the Torah's laws." No matter; the king would correct these deficiencies, acting in the name of political order. The secular authority, in short, has one sphere of authority, religious leaders another; and the former need not always give way to the latter in cases of conflict. The aims of Torah law may be more elevated, but the aims of secular law may be more urgent. Sometimes efforts to achieve a spiritually good life must yield to the necessity of preserving life itself.[4]

Once the legitimacy of two authorities, one secular, the other religious, was accepted, a question necessarily arose concerning the relation between them. This question assumed particular urgency after the fall of the Jewish commonwealth and the dispersion of the Jews among the nations of the earth. Shmuel, an authority of the early Talmudic period, laid down a principle that became central to all subsequent discussion of this issue: "The law of the [secular] kingdom is law."

This might seem to give secular authority plenipotentiary power over the Jewish community subject to its jurisdiction. Over time, however, two important limitations emerged—one formal, the other substantive. In the *Mishneh Torah*, Maimonides articulated a version of the principle that we now call "equal protection," which he used to distinguish between genuine laws and arbitrary decrees:

> The general rule is: any law promulgated by the king to apply to everyone and not to one person alone is not deemed robbery. But whatever he takes from one particular person only, not in accordance with a law known to everyone but [rather] by doing violence to this person, is deemed robbery. [5]

To be valid, law must comply with the requirements of formal justice. When secular authority disregards these formal requirements, its exceeds its just powers and may be criticized, even resisted, if circumstances permit.

Alongside this formal restraint, there developed a substantive limitation on the content of secular law that Jews were required to obey. In the course of answering questions posed by Napoleon to the Jews of France, Ishmael of Modena observed that "all the [interpreters of Shmuel's principle] have written that as long as the laws of the kingdom do not contradict Torah law, we must abide by them."[6] But what does it mean to "contradict" the Torah? The maximalist interpretation would be that civil law contradicts the Torah if, and to the extent that, it deviates from Torah law. To say this, however, would be to undermine virtually all civil law, contradicting the intention of the basic principle.

The most widely accepted interpretation, historically and down to the present, is that civil law is valid when it "does not contravene an explicit statement of the Torah."[7] Civil law loses its claim to be obeyed if it commands something that the Torah forbids, or forbids something that the Torah commands. It does not follow, however, that traditional Jews are always required to disobey civil law when such conflicts arise. A few civil demands (such as mandatory idolatry) must be resisted, to the death if need be. In most cases, however, it is permissible to take into account the severity of the consequences of disobedience.

THE POLITICS OF TRADITIONAL
JUDAISM IN A LIBERAL DEMOCRACY

In most contemporary liberal democracies, these sharp, explicit conflicts are relatively rare. In the United States, especially, the "free exercise" clause of the First Amendment offers substantial protections to those seeking to live in accordance with the dictates of their faith. Traditional Jews therefore join many other communities of faith in urging an expansive reading of this constitutional language. In 1990, the Supreme Court handed down a decision that reduced protections for free exercise by lowering the standard that government must meet to justify legal interference with religious practices.[8] Traditional Jews participated in a broad coalition to resist and reverse this decision by enacting the "Religious Freedom Restoration Act" (RFRA). This proposal, adopted by the Congress and signed into law by President Clinton in late 1993, required government to show that its interference was made necessary by a "compelling" interest and that the proposed intervention represented the least intrusive means of promoting that interest. (The Supreme Court subsequently invalidated RFRA as a violation of the separation of powers, and the struggle continues.)

Liberal democracies can act in ways that either relax or exacerbate the conflict between civil and Torah law. A number of contemporary political philosophers resist the strategy of accommodation in favor of policies that emphasize the force of "civic" claims and that pursue aims thought to be broadly desirable, regardless of their impact on particular communities of faith. Brian Barry, a leading representative of this tendency, has recently published a book arguing that civil concerns nearly always take priority and that cultural and religious claims rarely constitute grounds for objection or accommodation. So, for example, the public demand to prevent (alleged) cruelty to animals suffices to warrant the legal suppression of current kosher slaughtering practices. This is not even a deprivation of religious liberty, Barry asserts, for the simple reason that "nobody is bound to eat meat. (Some Orthodox Jews are vegetarians.)"[9] Clearly, traditional Jews must oppose all arguments of this form and urge instead that liberal democracy rightly understood embodies a presumption in favor of wide religious liberty that is overridden only in the event of a severe clash between religious practices and fundamental human interests that the state must defend. The state may prevent human sacrifice, and it may require Jehovah's Witnesses to permit their children to receive life-saving blood transfusions. But in enacting a general prohibition against the consumption of alcohol or other drugs, it must not prevent their sacramental use.

While debates over conflicts between the demands of civil law and the requirements of faith are noisy, such conflicts are relatively rare. Much more usual is the opposite case, when civil law permits what Torah law forbids. Under these circumstances, traditional Jews face a dual challenge: they must do their best to insulate their own communities against the temptations of a permissive cultural environment, and they may do what seems prudently possible to foster changes in civil law that narrow the gap with (at least the spirit of) Torah law.

I remarked earlier that living traditions contain multiple interpretive possibilities and that the challenge facing traditional Jews is to find defensible interpretations of both authoritative Jewish texts and the U.S. Constitution that to the greatest extent possible closes the gap between the demands of faith and the demands of citizenship. A strategy that addresses this challenge has now come into view. Following the Gerondian view, traditional American Jews must reject theocracy, instead acknowledging the legitimacy of autonomous secular political institutions that parallel and complement religious authority. At the same time, traditional Jews should embrace an interpretation of U.S. constitutionalism that is "liberal" rather than "civic republican"—that is, a stance that sees the legitimate scope of democratic political power as limited by individual rights, chief among them the right of free religious conscience and free exercise of practices commanded by faith.

TERMS OF ENGAGEMENT

It remains to sketch the forms of political engagement that traditional American Jews may employ to implement the broad strategy of narrowing the gap between citizenship and religion. To begin with, some public issues raise concerns, common to all citizens, that can be addressed in purely secular terms. For example, it would have been inappropriate for traditional Jews to invoke principles drawn from Judaism as a basis for resolving *Bush v. Gore*. Whatever one ultimately concludes about that bitterly contested case, the argument should rest on U.S. law, the Constitution, and established practices of adjudication.

There are forms of civic engagement, however, that warrant a distinctively Jewish approach. For example, traditional Jews have an intense interest in sustaining a legal and regulatory environment conducive to halachic practices. They will seek to prevent government actions that impede these practices (for example, burdensome restraints on ritual slaughter). From time to time, they may even seek to involve the government in protecting the integrity of halachic practices—for example, by using truth in advertising statutes to thwart false representations about the kosher status of food products.

Most traditional Jews believe that they must if possible send their children to schools in which Jewish practices, interpretive traditions, and history are seriously and systematically taught alongside required secular subjects. For more than seventy-five years, the Constitution has been understood as protecting their right to do so. (The famous case of *Pierce v. Society of Sisters*, decided in 1925, declared it unconstitutional for the law of any state to prohibit parents from sending their children to private or parochial schools.) But it is one thing to have the right, quite another to be able to exercise it. Many families are hard-pressed to pay for a Jewish education, even with community support. Traditional Jews therefore have an interest in laws establishing school vouchers and in court decisions that vindicate their constitutionality.

Some may doubt that group self-interest is an adequate basis for public advocacy. One familiar interpretation of American constitutionalism—Madisonian pluralism—suggests that it is, so long as the group's pursuit of its agenda remains within legal bounds. From this standpoint, groups are not always obliged to adopt the "public interest"—the well-being of society as a whole—as their guiding star. For many (not all) purposes, the clash of interests among groups, coupled with the negotiations these conflicts make necessary—will produce satisfactory outcomes. In a context in which all groups are pursuing their self-interest, "Is it good for the Jews?" is an appropriate question.

It is not the only question, however. As a practical matter, effective public advocacy requires groups to link their self-interest to wider societal interests and public purposes. As a matter of principle, Jews are famously reminded to ask themselves, "If I am only for myself, what am I?" I would suggest that this question applies to Jews, not only as individuals, but also as a collectivity. There are broader interests—of our fellow citizens, of humanity, of all Creation—that traditional Jews are required to regard with utmost seriousness.

How are these broader interests to be ascertained? In determining what purposes we share with our fellow citizens, the Preamble to the Constitution is an excellent guide. We are joined together "to form a more perfect Union, establish Justice, insure domestic Tranquility, provide for the common defence, promote the general Welfare, and secure the Blessings of liberty to ourselves and our Posterity." We may argue about *how* to pursue these goods, but not *whether* to do so.

This hallowed constitutional language takes us only so far. Not only do we disagree about the best means to these preambular ends (Which crime bill will best promote domestic tranquility? What level of military spending is needed to provide adequately for the common defence?), but also about the best understanding of the ends themselves. Terms such as justice, welfare, and liberty are far from self-interpreting.

To clarify them, we may have recourse to the tradition of interpretation that has developed since the American colonial period. We quickly discover that there is no a single canonical tradition, but multiple and competing traditions, the relative strength of which varies over time. For example, "liberty" in the American tradition is often understood in individualistic and negative terms, as protection against external coercion. From time to time, however, liberty is understood more positively and collectively, as citizen participation in those activities that preserve our existence as a "free people." It was in that latter spirit that John F. Kennedy challenged his generation to "ask what you can do for your country."

Not only are there multiple interpretative traditions in American political thought; they appeal to different sources of authority. While some rest on secular Enlightenment philosophies, others draw unabashedly from religion. In particular, the influence of the Old Testament on the self-understanding and political thought of the Puritan colonists is a commonplace among historians, and the unfolding of the American Revolution only strengthened this outlook. "The finger of God," said clergyman Phillip Payson in 1782, "has indeed been so conspicuous in every stage of our glorious struggle, that it seems as if the wonders and miracles performed for Israel of old were repeated over anew for the American Israel, in our day."[10] The influence of this potent analogy extended to an understanding of community as covenantal, of Americans as a chosen people, and of North America as a special land endowed with religious significance. These ideas were passed down through the generations, reappearing from time to time in the American public square, most dramatically in the speeches of Ronald Reagan.

In light of this history, it would seem arbitrary to rule out of bounds, as violations of norms of appropriate public discourse, all efforts by traditional Jews to bring their tradition to bear on the understanding of American public questions. Still, it matters how Jews do this. There is a difference between what may be called the defensive and offensive uses of religion. It is one thing to use the constitutional category of religious free exercise to defend the right of traditional Jews to engage in practices that others may find objectionable or incomprehensible; quite another to use propositions drawn from traditional Judaism as a basis for laws binding on all members of American society, Jews and non-Jews alike. The latter is clearly a more delicate matter calling for the utmost clarity and restraint.

While deliberating on possible laws for a diverse democratic society, interlocutors stand under an obligation to seek mutual intelligibility, so far as possible. This means that adherents of a particular tradition should do their best to state their claims in the broadly "constitutional" language common to all citizens. Non-constitutional discourse should never be the first resort.

Still, some issues resist reduction to the concepts and categories of the constitution. In such cases, the adherents of a particular tradition must do all they can to translate their understanding into terms that non-adherents can understand. They will not always be able to accomplish this, but they stand under the permanent obligation to try. When non-adherents ask why they should agree to a proposal, they are bound to be dissatisfied with an answer of the form, "Because the Lord our God has commanded *us* to do such-and-so."

Non-adherents have every right to ask why they should consider themselves bound by rules seemingly binding only on members of a group to which they do not themselves belong.

There are three possible responses to this difficulty. One is to articulate what Jewish tradition calls the reasons for the commandments. For some Jewish thinkers—Maimonides chief among them—underlying every particular commandment is a general reason that can be articulated to others. If we are not able to explain a commandment, it is because we have not yet studied it well enough to reach discernment.[11] A more mainstream Talmudic position distinguishes between transparent ordinances (*mishpatim*) "which, had they not been laid down, ought to have been laid down" and opaque edicts (*hukkim*) which at least appear to be "senseless deeds," a product of Divine will which traditional Jews have no permission to doubt.[12] Within the framework of this distinction, we can say that traditional Jews may use ordinances but not edicts as the basis of public arguments in a diverse democratic society, because explanation of the ordinances rests on reasons in principle accessible to all.

A second response to the difficulty of employing tradition-based claims as the basis of public discourse is to argue that certain principles found within a particular tradition are in fact binding on all human beings. David Novak has forcefully argued that there is in fact a Jewish "natural law" teaching—the so-called "Noahide law." This does not mean that all human beings are bound by exactly the same practical norms. Indeed, he insists,

> one cannot say that Jewish natural law thinking in and of itself produces any independent norms. It functions at the level of principles, not at the level of specific rules themselves. Actual law is always positive law at work with authority in a specific, concrete human community in history. What natural law does is to provide certain general criteria in the form of a *conditio sine qua non* for the formulation of this positive law so that it can have truth value in the world. Thus it is the limit of the law, not its content.[13]

If this is correct, traditional Jews can at least argue that certain positive laws are beyond the pale, and they can do so on the basis of principles binding on all and in principle rationally accessible to all.

A third response is to acknowledge that while mutual intelligibility on the basis of shared universal principles is not always possible, there are nonetheless some circumstances in which the resort to tradition-based particularity is unavoidable. For example, the U.S. Constitution speaks repeatedly of "persons," but—fatefully—it does not define personhood. Some of the bitterest struggles in American history have been fought over the question, Who is a person and, therefore, guaranteed the full and equal protection of the law?

Because the Constitution is incomplete—not fully self-explicating—it not only permits but actually requires propositions drawn from outside the perimeter of strictly constitutional discourse to resolve some of the cases and controversies to which it gives rise. There is no basis for excluding traditional Jews, or for that matter the adherents of any faith, from participating in the public process through which a binding specification of constitutional concepts ultimately emerges.

There is, finally, a form of Jewish public engagement that both affirms communal particularity and reaches out to others across communal boundaries. For some purposes, traditional Jews in the United States consciously separate themselves from their fellow citizens, but they do not withdraw from participation in the nation. These Jews interpret and honor their commandments in full view of non-Jewish citizens. In so doing, they send a message about how best to live. As others receive and react to this message, a kind of implicit civic dialogue develops. This dialogue cannot yield quick, clear results about specific public issues, but over time it can help shape a general civic consciousness.

Maimonides often quoted Deuteronomy 4:6 on this point: all who hear the statutes given to the Jews will say, "surely this great community is a wise and understanding people." He interprets this to mean that "all the statutes will show to all the nations that they have been given with wisdom and understanding."[14] But how can this be unless they are not only given, but also accepted, with wisdom and understanding? Perhaps the highest form of Jewish civic engagement is to do our utmost, in speech and deed—with acts of justice and kindness and concern for all—to bear witness to the merits of what we have inherited.

NOTES

1. Ian Machin, *Disraeli* (London: Longman, 1995), p. 90.

2. Michael Walzer et al, eds., *The Jewish Political Tradition, Volume one: Authority* (New Haven: Yale University Press, 2000), p. 473.

3. *Ibid*, p. 475.

4. For these quotations from Gerondi, see Walzer et al., pp. 156-159. As an indication of Gerondi's enduring importance as the prime expositor of the "two authorities" view, note that Isaac Halevi Herzog argues for the rejection of British and Turkish law for the state of Israel through a critique of Gerondi's position.

5. Maimonides, *Mishneh Torah*, Laws of Robbery and Lost Property 5:14.

6. Walzer et al., p. 451.

7. Ovadyah Haddayah, "Does *Dina de-Malkhuta Dina* Apply to the State of Israel?," excerpted in Walzer et al., p. 477.

8. *Employment Division v. Smith* 110 S. Ct. 1595 (1990).

9. Brian Barry, *Culture and Equality* (Cambridge, MA: Harvard, 2001), pp. 40-45.

10. Quoted in Richard Vetterli and Gary Bryner, *In Search of the Republic: Public Virtue and the Roots of American Government* (Totowa, NJ: Rowman & Littlefield, 1987), p. 49.

11. See especially *The Guide of the Perplexed*, 3:26-27, 31.

12. BT Yoma 67b.

13. David Novak, *Natural Law in Judaism* (Cambridge: Cambridge University Press, 1998), p. 164.

14. See, for example, Maimonides, *The Guide of the Perplexed,* 3:31.

Chapter Thirteen

Jews, Muslims, and the Prospects for Pluralism (2004)

The question of the hour is whether Islamic fundamentalism can be compatible with democracy. Though important, that question is subordinate to another: whether Islamic fundamentalism can make its peace with religious pluralism. After all, a democratic majority could well bring a Shiite theocracy to power in Iraq. A wide variety of institutional forms, many of which do not resemble American constitutionalism, can express and secure respect for pluralism. If that respect is absent, however, nation-builders will have no choice but to enforce tolerance, or to abandon beleaguered minorities to their fate.

James Carroll puts it well: "The challenge for religions of all kinds, but perhaps especially for religions based on narratives of divine revelation, is to make positive assertions of faith that do not simultaneously denigrate the different tenets of faith held by others." Those who believe that there are many paths to God, or that it is not given to finite humans to know which is the right path to the Infinite God, will find it relatively easy to embrace religious pluralism.

Genuine fundamentalists cannot accept either of these beliefs. Fundamentalists may however believe that other faiths are on the same (right) path although they cannot reach the end—the one true faith. They may also believe that it is wrong to use coercion as an instrument of religious conversion.

Each of these beliefs finds textual support as well as opposition within Islam. For example, in the Koran (al-Baraqah 2:62) we find the following: "Verily, those who believe and those who are Jews and Christians and Sabians, whoever believes in Allah and the Last day and do righteous good deeds shall have their reward with their Lord; on them shall be no fear, nor shall they grieve." Much depends on the ability of the proponents of a genuinely Islamic pluralism to broaden public support for a generous and accommodating interpretation of their shared tradition.

Acceptance of pluralism comes more easily to religions that emphasize inner conviction, because they need to ask little of politics beyond being left alone. By contrast, religions that take the form of law, as do traditional forms of Judaism and Islam, are forced to take seriously the content of public law. The terms of engagement between religious law and public law then become critical.

Speaking broadly and schematically, there are three possible relations between political and religious authority. Political authority may be comprehensively dominant over religion and thus put it in the service of state power (for this reason it is often termed "civil"). Second, political and religious authority may coexist, each with authority over different aspects of communal life. (Maxims such as "Render unto Caesar what is Caesar's" create the basis for such a pluralist understanding.) Finally, religious authority may coincide with, or comprehensively dominate, political authority, yielding theocracy.

When it comes to theocracy, there are important historical differences between Judaism and Islam. I want to begin by reflecting on Henry Munson's retelling of the Maccabean revolt, which he treats, plausibly enough, as an archetype of what we now call fundamentalism. Breaching a long-standing modus vivendi between Jews and their Seleucid rulers, King Antiochus Epiphanes arrogantly and unwisely ordered Jews to violate their most sacred commandments. When one of the resisters, the priest Mattathias, fled Jerusalem, the king's men pursued him. Mattathias resorted to violence only after it became apparent that the government would allow him no refuge and would not permit faithful Jews to observe their commandments without persecution.

This sequence of events is instructive in several respects. In the first place, unlike the Ottomans and the Hapsburgs, Antiochus was not satisfied to rule over a culturally diverse empire. Instead, he embarked on an aggressive campaign of cultural homogenization, unrelated to the requisites of stable and secure rule, that ultimately triggered resistance. Second, Mattathias's revolt originated not as a thrust toward theocracy but as a desperate defensive measure. He may well have been seething with resentment against Seleucid rule throughout his life, but the evidence suggests that he was prepared to accept it, so long as the authorities did not interfere with Jewish practices. Once his revolt began, however, its aims expanded to include the de-Hellenization of the entire society.

While bearing in mind dissimilarities among different varieties of fundamentalism, I will hazard a generalization from the Maccabean story: We should distinguish between religious movements that are essentially *defensive* in nature and those that are *offensive*.

Defensive fundamentalist movements are content to withdraw from the arena of power, or to participate in it on equal terms with others, so long as they are free to practice their faith. They may not accept other faiths as equal to their own. They may deplore the copresence of "foreign" or "strange" gods within their political community. But they are prepared to accept competing practices, out of necessity, as the price for being left alone.

Offensive movements, by contrast, seek power to impose their way on others. Four characteristics of offensive fundamentalist movements render them especially dangerous: their outlook is intolerant; their stance, uncompromising; their aspirations, totalist; their tactics, latently if not actually violent. These are the movements that pluralist societies and those seeking to build such societies (as in Iraq) have good reason to fear, and must resist.

Taken literally, the authority established by the laws of Moses was theocratic and, if the Book of Judges is to be taken as history, was exercised theocratically for an extended period. Gideon famously refused the people's demand that he become king over Israel: "I will not rule over you myself; nor shall my son rule over you; the Lord alone shall rule over you" (Judges 8:23).

But in practice, the legal structures of traditional (rabbinic) Judaism developed over a period of nearly two millennia during which Jews were a nearly powerless minority in the states they inhabited. The religious practices, such as the rituals of the Temple, that presupposed Jewish sovereignty in Israel fell into desuetude and were not revived—even after the reestablishment of a Jewish state in Israel in 1947. In the meantime, Shmuel, an authority of the early Talmudic period, had laid down the principle that became central to all subsequent discussion: "The law of the kingdom is law." Civil law loses its claim to be obeyed only when it commands something that the Torah explicitly forbids, or forbids something that the Torah commands.

As the discussion of these matters developed during the Talmudic and medieval periods, kingship became not a particular form of political regime but rather a metaphor for secular government in general. Nissim Gerondi, a leader of the Barcelona Jewish community, argued explicitly for two "separate agencies"—one to render decisions on a range of civil matters in accordance with religious law, the other to uphold public order. The secular authority, he argued, had one sphere of authority, religious leaders another. The two spheres overlapped to some extent, and it was not incumbent on secular authority to yield in cases of conflict. Jews were required to resist secular authority—at the cost of their lives if need be—in only a handful of instances, such as mandatory idolatry. Otherwise, the law of the kingdom was binding, the Torah notwithstanding.

Throughout the medieval and early modern periods, Jewish populations sought to maximize communal autonomy and to minimize conflict between the law of secular authorities and the commandments of the Torah. Efforts to enforce the fundamentals of the religion were invariably *defensive,* never offensive. And when, after World War II, Israel was established, it was barely thinkable that the religious law developed over centuries of political marginality in the diaspora could serve as civil legislation for the new state. For the most part, Orthodox communities and political parties in Israel ranked other goals ahead of the aspiration to rest civil legislation on Torah law, in part because applying it to political power wielded by a Jewish majority might well require sweeping revisions in the content of that law.

Nikki Keddie reminds us that the total intertwining of religion and politics is rare in Muslim history, and that calls for codifying Islamic law as the law of the state are "distinctly modern." Still, we need to explain the receptivity of many contemporary Muslim populations to such ideas. I would suggest that in contrast to Talmudic law, Shariah (the Muslim religious law founded on the Koran and the conduct and statements of the Prophet) developed in an extended period during which Muslims wielded political power, often over populations that were overwhelmingly Muslim. The structure of that law thus reflects the expectation that it would have political as well as communal authority. As Khaled Abou El Fadl states, classical Muslim jurists described the best system of government as "the caliphate, based on Sharia'ah law [which] fulfills the criteria of justice and legitimacy and binds governed and governor alike." The idea of a secular state in which Shariah is both distinct from and subordinate to political authority stands in uneasy relation to this ideal, and many Muslims experience that idea as an alien (Western) imposition.

For example, in 1959, Iraq's new revolutionary ruler, General Abd al-Karim Qasim, promulgated a Code of Personal Status that contradicted Shariah in areas such as polygamy and inheritance. Clerical resistance to the Code helped undermine General Qasim's regime, and the repeal of the Code was among the first acts of the new government that took power in 1963 following a successful coup. Calls to rest civil law on Shariah and to recognize the autonomy of religious judges have a resonance in Islamic communities without parallel for most Jews, no matter how observant.

It would be too hasty to conclude, however, that Islamic fundamentalism must entail some form of theocracy or always take a violent and intolerant form. There are a number of political arrangements that might express an Islamic outlook without ceasing to respect pluralism. Clearly, Ataturk's severe anti-clericalism is not one of them. Nor is an American-style separation of church and state.

But one might well imagine an Islamic version of the Netherlands, a state in which a number of different faiths enjoy public funding and public standing, especially in the arena of education. Another possibility is a new version of the multi-confessional structure of the Ottoman Empire (reproduced to some degree in Israel), in which a dominant religious group shares civic space with other faiths that enjoy substantial autonomy and authority, especially over family law.

In short, there is no reason, other than the perennial *libido dominandi,* why a moderate official "establishment" of Islam need eventuate in religious persecution and repression. As Noah Feldman, author of *After Jihad: America and the Struggle for Islamic Democracy,* has written:

> If many in the West cannot imagine democracy without separation of church and state, many in the Muslim world find it impossible to imagine legitimate democracy with it. Fortunately, democracy does not require an absolute divide between religion and political authority. Liberty of conscience is an indispensable requirement of free government—but an established religion that does not coerce religious belief and that treats religious minorities as equals may be perfectly compatible with democracy.

In this regard, the trajectory of Iran since 1979 is instructive. Ayatollah Khomeini's rhetoric responded both to the cultural dislocations of modernity and to imperialism's affront to national pride. Over time, however, the majority of Iranians began to react against what they experienced as theocratic oppression. In their eyes, what initially presented itself as a cure had become part of the disease. For all we know, ordinary citizens in Saudi Arabia are equally impatient with the severity of Wahhabi fundamentalism. The difference is that the Iranian Constitution allows for elections that express popular sentiment and that influence the distribution of political power.

There is thus reason to hope that, given time, the exposure of Islamic regimes to the culture of modernity and to institutions of democratic accountability will produce a tolerable degree if not of respect at least of liberty for diverse faiths and ways of life. In contemporary circumstances, that liberty is the principal requisite of political decency.

Bibliography

Amato, Paul R. and Alan Booth. *A Generation at Risk: Growing Up in an Era of Family Upheaval*. Cambridge, MA: Harvard University Press, 1997.

Apple, R. W., Jr. "Public Rates Bush Highly But Sees Mostly Style." *New York Times*, 20 April 1989, p. B12.

Barnes, James A. "Florida Snowball." *National Journal*, 29 July 1989, p. 1959.

Barnes, James A. "Politics After Webster." *National Journal*, 12 August 1989, pp. 2044–48.

Baym, Nancy K. "The Emergence of Community in Computer-Mediated Communication." Steven G. Jones, ed. *Cybersociety: Computer-Mediated Communication and Community*. Thousand Oaks, CA: Sage, 1995.

Bender, Thomas. *Community and Social Change in America*. Baltimore: Johns Hopkins University Press, 1982

Bennett, Stephen E. "Why Young Americans Hate Politics, and What We Should Do About It." *PS* 30, no 1, March 1997, pp. 47–53.

Bimber, Bruce. "The Internet and Political Transformation: Populism, Community, and Accelerated Pluralism." *Polity* 31, no. 1 (Fall 1998): 133-160.

Brown, Peter A. "Democrats Concealed Study of How to Win White Votes." *Scripps-Howard News Service*, 17 April 1989.

Chase-Lansdale, P. Lindsey, Andrew J. Cherlin, and Kathleen Kiernan. "The Long-Term Effects of Parental Divorce on the Mental Health of Young Adults: A Developmental Perspective." *Child Development* 66 (1995): 1614–1634.

Cherlin, Andrew J. *Marriage, Divorce, Remarriage*. Cambridge, MA: Harvard University press, 1992.

Cherlin, Andrew J., P. Lindsey Chase-Lansdale, and Christine McRae. "Effects of Divorce on Mental Health Through the Life Course." *Hopkins Population Center Papers on Population* WP 97-1 (February 1997).

Cherlin, Andrew J., Kathleen Kiernan, and P. Lindsey Chase-Lansdale. "Parental Divorce in Childhood and Demographic Outcomes in Young Adulthood." *Demography* 32, no. 3 (August 1995): pp. 299–318.

Coleman, John A. "Introduction: A Tradition Celebrated, Reevaluated, and Applied." *One Hundred Years of Catholic Social Thought*. Maryknoll, NY: Orbis Books, 1991.

Coleman, John A.. "Neither Liberal nor Socialist: The Originality of Catholic Social Teaching." *One Hundred Years of Catholic Social Thought*. Maryknoll, NY: Orbis Books, 1991.

Community Works: The Revival of Civil Society in America. E. J. Dionne Jr., ed. Washington, DC: Brookings, 1998.

Crenshaw, Albert B. "For Two-Income Couples, More Reasons Not to Get Tied." *Washington Post*, 24 August 1997, p. H1

De Tocqueville, Alexis. *Democracy in America*. George Lawrence, trans. New York: Harper & Row, 1966.

DeNardo, James. "Turnout and the Vote: The Joke's on the Democrats," *American Political Science Review* 74, no. 2 (June 1980): pp. 406–20.

DiFonzo, J. Herbie. *Beneath the Fault Line: The Popular and Legal Culture of Divorce in Twentieth-Century America*. Charlottesville: University Press of Virginia, 1997.

"Digital Democracy" organized by the National Research Council (June 12, 2000, Washington, DC).

Dionne, E. J., Jr. "If Nonvoters Had Voted: Same Winner, But Bigger." *New York Times*, 21 November 1989.

Dionne, E. J., Jr. "Poll Finds Ambivalence on Abortion Persists in U.S." *New York Times*, 3 August 1989.

Divorce Reform at the Crossroads. Stephen D. Sugarman and Herma Hill Kay, eds. New Haven: Yale University Press, 1990.

"Modern Catholic Social Thought." Judith A. Dwyer, ed. *The New Dictionary of Catholic Social Thought*. Collegeville, MN: The Liturgical Press.

Edley, Christopher, Jr. and Gene Sperling. "Have We Really 'Done Enough' for Civil Rights?" *Washington Post*, 25 June 1989, p. B1.

Edsall, Thomas. "Racial Forces Battering Southern Democrats." *Washington Post*, 25 June 1989, p. A6.

Ehrenhalt, Alan. *The Lost City: Discovering the Forgotten Virtues of Community in the Chicago of the 1950s*. New York: Basic, 1995.

Ehrenhalt, Alan. "Where Have All the Followers Gone?" E. Dionne, ed. *Community Works: The Revival of Civil Society in America*. Washington, DC: Brookings, 1998.

Embryo Experimentation. Peter Singer et al., ed. Cambridge: Cambridge University Press, 1990.

Erikson, Robert S. "Economic Conditions and the Presidential Vote." *American Political Science Review*, 82, no. 2 (June 1989): pp. 567–73.

Esposito, John L. *Women in Muslim Family Law,* 2nd Edition. Syracuse, NY: Syracuse University Press, 2001.

"Event Driven News Audiences: Internet News Takes Off." Pew Research Center for People and the Press. 8 June 1998.

Feeney, Susan. "Hostile Student Views at LSU Have Two Top Demos Rattled." *New Orleans Times-Picayune*, 9 March 1989.

Friedman, Lawrence M. *The Republic of Choice: Law, Authority, and Culture*. Cambridge, MA: Harvard University Press, 1990.

Fullinwider, Robert K., ed. *Civil Society, Democracy, and Civic Renewal*. Lanham, MD: Rowman & Littlefield, 1999.

Furstenberg, Frank F., Jr. and Andrew J. Cherlin. *Divided Families: What Happens to Children When Parents Part?* Cambridge, MA: Harvard University Press, 1991.

Galston, William. "Divorce America Style." *The Public Interest* 124 (Summer 1996): pp. 12–26.

Galston, William. *Liberal Pluralism*. New York: Cambridge University Press, 2002.

Galston, William. *Liberal Purposes: Goods, Virtues, and Diversity in the Liberal State*. New York: Cambridge University Press, 1991.

Galston, William. *The Practice of Liberal Pluralism*. New York: Cambridge University Press, 2004.

Germond, Jack W. and Jules Whitcover. "Abortion Issue Giving Democrats Big Opening." *National Journal*, 12 August 1989, p. 2056.

Germond, Jack W. and Jules Whitcover. *Whose Broad Stripes and Bright Stars? The Trivial Pursuit of the Presidency 1998*. New York: Warner Books, 1989.

Goodwin, Doris Kearns. *The Fitzgeralds and the Kennedys: An American Saga*. New York: St. Martin's, 1987.

Gordon, Sarah Barringer. *The Mormon Question: Polygamy and Constitutional Conflict in Nineteenth Century America*. Chapel Hill: University of North Carolina Press, 2002.

Gourevitch, Philip. "Damage Control," *The New Yorker*, 26 July 2004, p. 55.

Guterbock, Thomas M. and John C. Fries, "Maintaining America's Social Fabric: The AARP Survey of Civic Involvement." University of Virginia: Center for Survey Research, 1997.

Hall, Bob and Barry Yeoman. "What Happened November 8th?" *Southern Exposure*, Spring 1989.

Hehir, J. Bryan. "The Right and Competence of the Church in the American Case." John A. Coleman, ed. *One Hundred Years of Catholic Social Thought*. Maryknoll, NY: Orbis Books, 1991.

Honeycutt, Amanda A. *Marriage, Divorce, and the Impacts on Children: Using State Laws to Identify Causal Relationships*. Ph.D. Dissertation, Department of Economics, University of Maryland, College Park, 1997.

Kamarck, Elaine Ciulla. "Cutting in on Campaign Cash." *Newsday*, 12 February 1989, Ideas Section, p. 1.

Kamarck, Elaine Ciulla. "Pols Who'd Rather Switch Than Fight." *Newsday*, 21 August 1989.

Kamarck, Elaine Ciulla. "Where Have All the Voters Gone?" *Newsday*, 12 September 1988.

Kamarck, Elaine Ciulla and William A. Galston, "A Progressive Family Policy for the 1990s." *Mandate for Change*. Will Marshall and Martin Schram, eds. New York: Berkley Books, 1993.

Kaplan, Robert D. "Travels into America's Future." *The Atlantic Monthly* 282:2, August 1998, 37–61.

Kirkpatrick, Jeane J. *The New Presidential Elite: Men and Women in National Politics.* New York: Russell Sage Foundation, 1976.

Ladd, Everett Carll, Jr. "The Twentysomethings: 'Generation Myths.' Revisited" *The Public Perspective* 5:2, January/February 1994, pp. 14–18.

Ladd, Everett Carll, Jr. *Where Have All the Voters Gone? The Fracturing of America's Political Parties* 2d ed. New York: Norton, 1982.

Lengle, James. "Presidential Primaries and Representation." *Presidential Politics: Readings on Nominations and Elections.* James I. Lengle and Byron E. Shafer, eds. 2nd ed. New York: St. Martin's Press, 1983.

Lukas, Anthony. *Common Ground: A Turbulent Decade in the Lives of Three American Families.* New York: Knopf, 1985.

Machin, Ian. *Disraeli.* London: Longman, 1995

Mann, Thomas E. *Unsafe at any Margin: Interpreting Congressional Elections.* Washington, DC: American Enterprise Institute, 1978.

Mantovani, Giuseppe. *New Communication Environments: From Everyday to Virtual.* London: Taylor & Francis, 1996.

Maraniss, Dave. "In Wright's Texas Alliances Are Shifting." *Washington Post,* 10 August 1989, p. A3.

Marvin, Carolyn. *When Old Technologies Were New: Thinking About Electric Communications in the Late Nineteenth Century.* New York: Oxford University Press, 1988.

Maynard-Moody, Steven. "Managing Controversies over Science: The Case of Fetal Research." *Journal of Public Administration Research and Theory* 5 (1995): 10.

McLanahan, Sara and Gary Sandefur. *Growing Up with a Single Parent: What Hurts, What Helps?* Cambridge, MA: Harvard University Press, 1994.

McLaughlin, Margaret, Kerry K. Osborne, and Christine B. Smith, "Standards of Conduct on Usenet." Steven G. Jones, ed. *Cybersociety: Computer-Mediated Communication and Community.* Thousand Oaks, CA: Sage, 1995.

Miller, Warren E. and J. Merrill Shanks. *The New American Voter.* Cambridge, MA: Harvard University Press, 1996.

Norris, Pippa. "Who Surfs? New Technology, Old Voters, and Virtual Democracy in America," in Elaine Ciulla Kamarck and Joseph S. Nye, Jr., eds. *Democracy.com?: Governance in a Networked World.* Hollis, NH: Hollis Publishing, 1999.

Novak, David. *Natural Law in Judaism.* Cambridge: Cambridge University Press, 1998.

O'Brien, David. "A Century of Catholic Social Teaching." John A. Coleman, ed. *One Hundred Years of Catholic Social Thought.* Maryknoll, NY: Orbis Books, 1991.

Oreskes, Michael. "Civil Rights Act Leaves Deep Mark on the American Political Landscape." *New York Times,* 2 July 1989.

Ornstein, Norman J., Thomas E. Mann, and Michael J. Malbin. *Vital Statistics on Congress, 1987–1988.* Washington, DC: American Enterprise Institute/Congressional Quarterly, 1987.

Ostrom, Elinor. *Governing the Commons: The Evolution of Institutions for Collective Action.* New York: Cambridge University Press, 1990.

Parkman, Allen M. *No-Fault Divorce: What Went Wrong?* Boulder, CO: Westview Press, 1992.

Perry, James M. "Republican Campaign Is Paying Off as Conservative Democrats Make Switch in South." *Wall Street Journal*, 14 August 1989, p. A10.

Phelps, Edmund S. *Rewarding Work: How to Restore Participation and Self-Support to Free Enterprise*. Cambridge, MA: Harvard University Press, 1997.

Postman, Neil. *Technopoly: The Surrender of Culture to Technology*. New York: Vintage, 1993.

Putnam, Robert D. "Bowling Alone." *Journal of Democracy* 1, January 1995, pp. 65–78.

Rahn, Wendy, John Brehm, and Neil Carlson. "National Elections as Institutions for Generating Social Capital." Theda Skocpol and Morris P. Fiorina, eds. *Civic Engagement in American Democracy*. Washington, DC: Brookings, 1999.

Rauch, Jonathan. *Demosclerosis: The Silent Killer of American Government*. New York: Times Books, 1994.

Reider, Jonathan. *Canarsie: The Jews and Italians of Brooklyn Against Liberalism*. Cambridge: Harvard University Press.

Rosenstone, Steven J. "Explaining the 1984 Presidential Election." *Brookings Review*, Winter 1985, pp. 25-32.

Rosenstone, Steven J. *Forecasting Presidential Elections*. New Haven, CT: Yale University Press, 1983.

Scott, Elizabeth S. "Rational Decision-Making about Marriage and Divorce." *Virginia Law Review* 76:1 (1990): pp. 9–94.

Shapiro, Andrew L. *The Control Revolution: How the Internet is Putting Individuals in Charge and Changing the World We Know*. New York: PublicAffairs, 1999.

Skocpol, Theda. "Advocates without Members: The Recent Transformation of American Civic Life." Theda Skocpol and Morris P. Fiorina, eds. *Civic Engagement in American Democracy*. Washington, DC: Brookings, 1999.

Skocpol, Theda. "A Partnership with American Families." *The New Majority: Toward a Popular Progressive Politics*. Stanley B. Greenberg and Theda Skocpol, eds. New Haven: Yale University Press, 1997.

Skocpol, Theda and Morris P. Fiorina, eds. *Civic Engagement in American Democracy*. Washington, DC: Brookings, 1999.

Snyder, Joel. "Get Real," *Internet World* 7, 2 (1996): pp. 92–94.

Sunstein, Cass R. *Republic.com*. Princeton, NJ: Princeton University Press, 2001.

Van Alstyne, Marshall and Erik Brynjolfsson, "Electronic Communities: Global Village of Cyberbalkans?" MIT Sloan School, March 1997.

Vetterli, Richard and Gary Bryner. *In Search of the Republic: Public Virtue and the Roots of American Government*. Totowa, NJ: Rowman & Littlefield, 1987.

Virtual Culture: Identity & Communication in Cybersociety. Steven G. Jones, ed. Thousand Oaks, CA: Sage, 1997.

The Jewish Political Tradition, volume one: Authority. Michael Walzer et al., eds. New Haven, CT: Yale University Press, 2000.

Watson, Nessim. "Why We Argue about Virtual Community: A Case Study of the Phish.Net Fan Community." Steven G. Jones, ed. *Virtual Culture: Identity & Communication in Cybersociety*. Thousand Oaks, CA: Sage, 1977.

Williams, Dr. Linda F. "'88 Election Results: Problems and Prospects for Black Politics." Joint Center for Political Studies, Washington, DC.

Witcover, Jules. *Party of the People: A History of the Democrats*. New York: Random House, 2003.

Wolfe, Alan. *One Nation, After All: What Middle-Class Americans Really Think About: God, Country, Family, Racism, Welfare, Immigration, Homosexuality, Work, The Right, The Left, and Each Other*. New York: Viking, 1998.

Wolfe, Alan. "The Moral Meanings of Work." *The American Prospect* (September/October 1997): p. 87.

Wolfinger, Raymond E. and Steven J. Rosenstone. *Who Votes?* New Haven, CT: Yale University Press, 1980.

Yankelovich, Daniel. "How Changes in the Economy Are Reshaping American Values," in Henry J. Aaron, Thomas E. Mann, and Timothy Taylor, eds. *Values and Public Policy*. Washington, DC: Brookings, 1994.

Zill, Nicholas, Donna R. Morrison, and Mary J. Coiro. "Long-Term Effects of Parental Divorce on Parent-Child Relationships, Adjustment, and Achievement in Young Adulthood." *Journal of Family Psychology* 7, 1 (1993): pp. 91–103.

Index

About the Author

William A. Galston is Saul Stern Professor, School of Public Policy, University of Maryland, director of the Institute for Philosophy and Public Policy, and founding director of the Center for Information and Research on Civic Learning and Engagement (CIRCLE). He has participated in five presidential campaigns and served in the White House as Deputy Assistant to President Clinton for Domestic Policy, 1993–1995. His most recent books are *Liberal Pluralism* (2002) and *The Practice of Liberal Pluralism* (2004).